Linda,
Thank you for your [?]...
to our book. Your friendship has spanned decades! What a treasure!
Liz & Mark

WHO DO YOU SAY THAT I Am?

❦

40 POEMS OF PRAISE
AND INSPIRATION

God is always with you. Be still and enjoy His presence!

Liz & Mark Descant

MARCUS DESCANT AND LIZ DESCANT

Marc Descant

2023

Who Do You Say That *I Am*?

❦

40 POEMS OF PRAISE
AND INSPIRATION

RECALLING THE LIFE AND
WORKS OF JESUS CHRIST

COMPLETE WITH
STUDY GUIDE

Copyright © 2023 Marcus Descant and Liz Descant
All rights reserved
First Edition

PAGE PUBLISHING
Conneaut Lake, PA

First originally published by Page Publishing 2023

ISBN 978-1-6624-8476-6 (pbk)
ISBN 978-1-6624-8477-3 (digital)

Printed in the United States of America

CONTENTS

A Book for All Christians vii
Introduction..ix
How to Use This Book...xi
   40.. xv

Chapter 1:   The Birth of Jesus..1
   Prayer to My Guardian Angel..3
   A Christmas Child 7
   God Is Love...11
   In Praise of Saint Joseph 17
   The Holy Family 21
   The Christ...25

Chapter 2:   The Teachings and Miracles of Jesus Christ 31
   A Voice from the Heart 33
   God's Will...37
   His Holy Word 43
   In the Palm of His Hand..47
   Jesus in the Temple...53
   King of Heaven and Earth..57
   My Brother 61
   Temptation 65
   The Little One 69
   The Saints 73
   The Storm...77
   Miracles 81

Chapter 3:   The Holy Eucharist...87
   A Prayer for Priests 89
   Consecration Prayer 93
   The Holy Eucharist...97

Chapter 4: The Crucifixion 105
    Heart-to-Heart 107
    I Thirst 111
    Love 115
    It Is Finished 119
    A Holy Death 125

Chapter 5: Tribute to the Blessed Mother and Her Grief 131
    Grief 133
    Mary, Queen of Heaven 137
    Prayer to Our Lady 143
    The Woman 147

Chapter 6: The Resurrection 153
    The Resurrection 155
    Welcome Home 161
    The Soul 165
    The Kingdom 169
    Heaven 173

Chapter 7: The Descent of the Holy Spirit 179
    Come, Holy Spirit 181
    The Spirit of God 185
    Thank You, Holy Spirit 189
    My Life 193
References 197

A BOOK FOR ALL CHRISTIANS

Pope John Paul II, also known as the pilgrim for ecumenism, advocated for unity among all Christians. This was Christ's desire as He carried His cross to Calvary. As He walked, He prayed "that they may all be one, even as you Father are in me and I in you, that they also may be in us so that the world may believe that You have sent me."

This book is dedicated to all Christians who want to develop a relationship with the Lord. To those people who already have that relationship, we pray that it will be strengthened.

INTRODUCTION

I have been writing prayer poems for almost forty years. Over the years, many people read the poems and many kept asking us to publish a book. Well, one reason we haven't is that neither my wife, Liz, nor I know anything about publishing a book! As time went on, people kept asking. So we finally decided to check into publishing a book. We did, and here we are!

This book is a collection of forty prayer poems that I have written over a span of almost forty years. My wife and I decided to take the book a step further and develop a study guide to go with each poem. The study guide is designed to have the reader dig deeper into the content of the poetry and how it relates to our Christian beliefs.

These poems are written for all Christians regardless of your denomination. Using the study guides, the reader can broaden their knowledge base of Christian beliefs by interactive activities, such as locating scripture, forming opinions, discussing, creative writing, and completion of additional activities.

When choosing the layout for this book, we wanted the order of the poems to tell a story. The book comes together in seven chapters recalling the life and works of Jesus Christ, beginning with the birth of Jesus and ending with the descent of the Holy Spirit.

We called on a few friends to assist with the study guides. These friends were from several different Christian denominations. They were asked to submit a few questions that would be appropriate for the poetry and help the reader learn more about their Christian beliefs. The names of the resource people are listed in the bibliography of the book.

We were both overwhelmed and humbled by the response we received. We took much of this information and developed the study guides. The questions in the study guides align with the contents of the poems. We are forever grateful to those people who answered our call for help!

This book is your book, and enjoy it the way you would like!

HOW TO USE THIS BOOK

Who Do You Say That **I Am**? is a collection of forty prayer poems that recall the life and works of Jesus Christ. The story is told in seven chapters. The number 7 in the Bible has always had a special meaning. The number 7 represents *completeness* and *perfection*. We pray that this book will represent completeness and perfection to honor and give glory to our Lord.

The seven chapters are the following:

> The Birth of Jesus
> The Teachings and Miracles of Jesus Christ
> The Holy Eucharist
> The Crucifixion
> Tribute to the Blessed Mother and Her Grief
> The Resurrection
> The Descent of the Holy Spirit

This book is to be enjoyed. You may use this book individually or in small groups, such as in Bible study, in prayer groups, or in educational settings. You may enjoy reading only the poetry, or you may prefer to include the study guide as well. You have many options.

In developing the study guides, we thought it was important for the book to be interactive and include a variety of questions and activities. By taking this approach, the reader is actively involved and more learning occurs. The content of the study guides aligns with the content of the poems. The guides are divided into four parts: *A, B, C,* and *D*. You may choose how you want to use the study guides.

Your answers are your answers. You are not preparing for a test. This is YOUR book. Use it like YOU want!

You will need the following items to complete the study guide: this book, your Bible, a notebook and/or journal, writing tools, and art supplies. Access to a computer would be great as well as a way to listen to music.

In each chapter, you will find questions that ask you to locate information in the Bible, questions about your opinion based on your knowledge, and creative writing.

Throughout each chapter, you will find a few questions related to science, math, and geography. After each poem, you are asked to play and sing your favorite songs about the poem title. You also may need a CD player or other instrument for playing music. YouTube will come in very handy here! Don't hesitate to use the search engines on your computers, such as yahoo.com or google.com and other resources to assist you in locating information.

As a culminating activity for each chapter, you are asked to use your favorite art medium, such as drawing, painting, photography, mixed media, printmaking, and sculpture to create an original design that represents the poems in that chapter.

The amount of information that could be used in each chapter is endless. At the end of each chapter, you will find additional pages to record notes or other important information.

Choose a few activities, or do them all. Have fun, and enjoy your book!

WHO IS JESUS TO YOU?

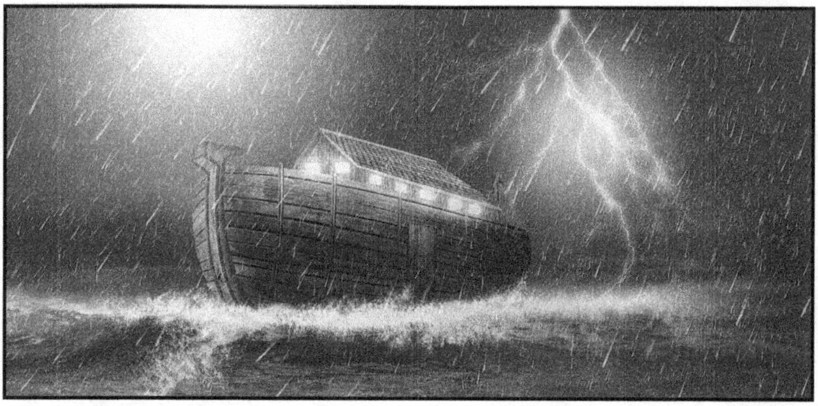

40

As I sit here pondering over my time,
The number 40 comes to my mind.

For 40 days, Moses stayed away.
Coming back, he found his people had gone astray.

The Hebrew people spent much time alone.
After 40 years, they found a place to call home.

In the time of Noah, he brought his family together.
The others on earth were destroyed by bad weather.

After 40 days, rising from the dead,
Jesus sent the Holy Spirit to move His people ahead.

40

Study Guide A

1. What is the significance of the number *40* in the Bible?

2. Moses left his people for *40* days. How had his people gone astray during those *40* days? Find your answer in Exodus 32:1–8 and document.

3. Why didn't God allow the Israelites to reach the Promised Land sooner? Document your answer. How does this relate to people of today?

Study Guide B

4. What chapter in the book of Genesis speaks of the flood that lasted *40* days and *40* nights? Document your answer.

5. What is Pentecost Sunday, and what does it represent? Find this in scripture and document.

Study Guide C

6. The number *40* is mentioned in the Bible over 140 times. A few of them are mentioned in this poem. How many more can you find? Document the scripture where your answers are found.

Study Guide D

7. Read the poem "40." Circle the stanza that moves you. Why does it stir your heart?

8. Read the poem again. Circle a few words that stand out to you. Write a prayer to Jesus, and include these words.

Record the prayer in your journal to complete your personal book of prayers.

9. Play and sing your favorite songs or hymns about *40*.

Art Activity

Use your favorite art medium to complete an original design containing the many representations of *40* in the Bible. Have fun!

CHAPTER 1

The Birth of Jesus

O HOLY NIGHT

"*I Am*...Jesus, the son of God."

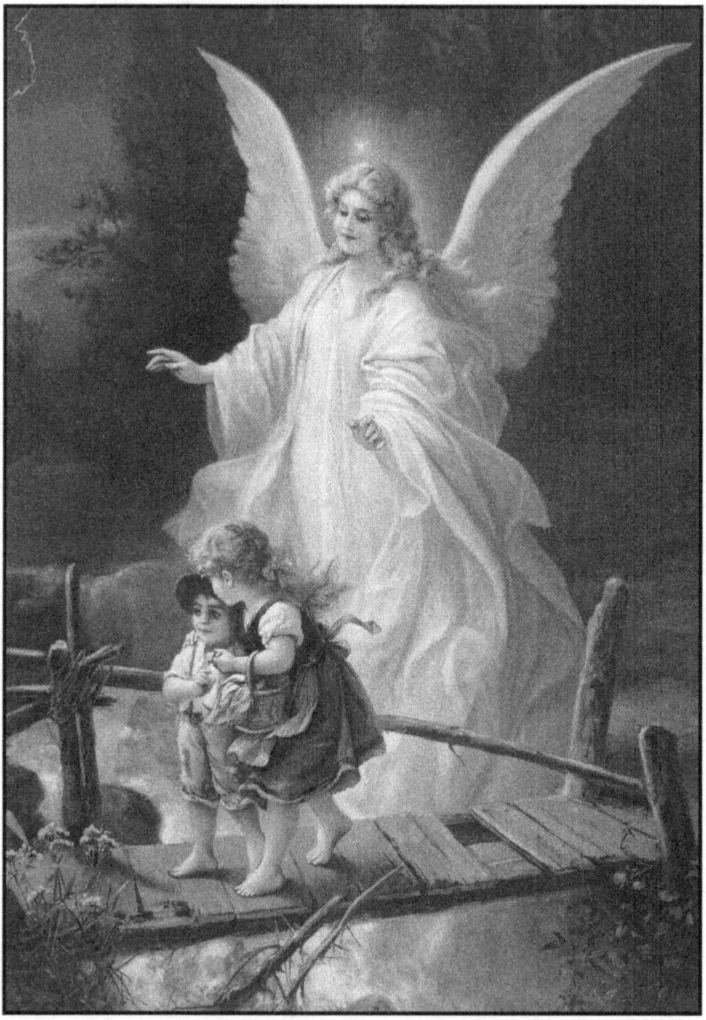

Prayer to My Guardian Angel

O angel of light, O spirit so bright
Show us the way in this darkness of night.

Protect our souls during the coming storm
And from all those things that can cause us harm.

Please lead us to our mother's side
For, to Jesus through Mary, our hearts will reside.

Prayer to My Guardian Angel

Study Guide A

1. Who are guardian angels?

2. Where can you find the scripture about guardian angels in the Bible?

3. Read in the Bible Psalm 91:10–12, Hebrews 1:13–14, and Mark 13:27. What do these scriptures say about angels?

Study Guide B

4. Explain the "angel of light" in this poem. What does it mean to you?

5. What does the "spirit so bright" in this poem mean to you?

6. Do you think the meanings are related to each other?

7. How does the poem "Prayer to My Guardian Angel" apply to you and your life?

Study Guide C

8. Can you remember a time when you felt the presence of an angel in your life? Explain.

9. Read Psalm 91:11–12, Matthew 18:10, and Acts 12:9–15. Explain the concept of angels and guardian angels.

10. What other scriptures about angels stand out to you?

11. Read Revelation 12:7–9, Tobit 12:13–15, and Luke 1:26–33. Who are the three archangels? Explain each one. What were their functions as archangels?

Study Guide D

12. What does science say about angels?

13. Where were angels and archangels present in the Old Testament, and where are they found in the New Testament?

14. Who were the seven fallen angels? Why were they cast out of heaven? Who was their leader?

15. Read this poem. Circle the stanza that stands out to you. Why does it move you?

16. Read this poem. Circle a few words that stand out to you. Write a prayer to Jesus and include those words. Record the prayer in your journal to complete your personal book of prayers.

17. Play and sing your favorite songs or hymns about angels.

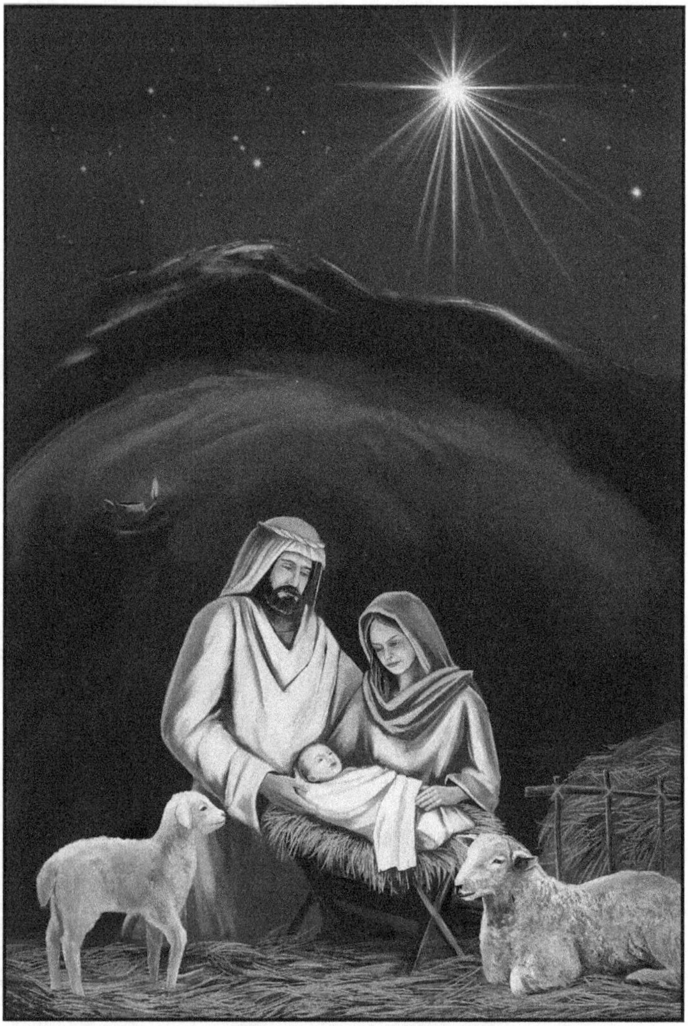

A Christmas Child

On one cold and dark winter night
An angel of the Lord,
Led Mary and Joseph
on a flight.

The night was cold
With no place to stay,
They ended up in a barn
That was full of hay.

Mary was with child
Whose name was Jesus,
He was born, and by His birth
He would save us.

In the barn
There was a manger,
It was not fit
Even for a stranger.

Because of His humility
Shown by His birth,
It opened the door
To save everyone on earth.

A Christmas Child

Study Guide A

1. Do you think God was a vision or a dream? What does the Scripture say? What is your opinion?

2. Why did Jesus come to earth? Where in the book of Luke can you find this?

3. Read Micah 5:1–5 and Matthew 2:4–6 of the Bible. Where was it prophesied that the savior would be born? Why was the savior to be born there?

4. Who were some of the prophets that predicted the savior's birth?

5. Read Matthew 1:18–24. Explain Joseph's reaction when he learned that Mary was expecting a child. What was Joseph's plan? Did he follow through with his plan? Why or why not?

Study Guide B

6. How do you think Mary and Joseph felt being away from home with the imminent birth of a child and nowhere to go?

7. Do you relate more to a young girl's trusting assent to the divine message of God, or do you relate to Joseph's desperate quest for safety and protection for his vulnerable wife? Explain.

8. Where was Jesus born? Describe the area.

9. If you were to map out the journey of the magi to Bethlehem, what would it look like? How long do you think it took for

the journey? What were the travel conditions? What gifts did the magi bring? Why?

Study Guide C

10. Which Gospel is the only Gospel that mentions the magi as "the three wise men"? What does the Scripture say about them?

11. Read in the book of Luke 2:8–16. Describe a manger. What were the two uses for mangers during these times? How and why were mangers used for sacrificial lambs?

12. Which of the four gospels do we read most about the Nativity at Christmas?

13. How is the poem "A Christmas Child" linked to both the Old Testament and the New Testament? Document your answer with a scripture.

Study Guide D

14. Read this poem "A Christmas Child." Circle the paragraph that means the most to you. Why does it stir your heart?

15. Read this poem again. Circle a few words that stand out to you. Write a prayer to Jesus and include these words. Record your prayer in your journal to complete your personal book of prayers.

16. Select five of your favorite activities to do with your family during the Christmas season. Discuss with your family why you do each one.

17. Play and sing your favorite Christmas carols or hymns.

God is love

God Is Love

Even though our Father is in heaven above
We can rest assure He sends down His love,

He sent His Son down to earth
Giving us hope by Jesus's birth.

He loves us so much as we have seen before
He then sent His spirit to open another door.

The Holy Spirit is the name we call
He is a blessing for us after the fall.

We then pray to the Holy Trinity to help us in this life
To give us the grace and hope, and help us with our daily strife.

God Is Love

Study Guide A

1. Read in the book of Genesis chapter 1. When is the spirit of God first mentioned in the Bible?

2. Where in the Bible does God give us an indication that there is more than one part to His being?

3. How is Adam and Eve related to the "fall of mankind" and to you?

4. This poem "God Is Love" mentions the "blessing after the fall." What does that mean to you?

Study Guide B

5. Read in the book of Genesis chapter 3. Explain how the "fall of mankind" affects future generations.

6. Read in the book of Romans chapter 5. Explain God's free and unconditional love. What does that mean to you?

7. Read in Isaiah 43:1–4. How does this scripture explain God's love for us?

8. In Luke 12:7, how does this passage describe a more particular love that God has for you? Explain.

Study Guide C

9. Read in the books of Matthew 25:31–40 and Isaiah 58:1–9 in the Bible. What are the seven Corporal Works of Mercy? How can we practice the Corporal Works of Mercy to show

love to others just as God has shown love to us? Please write examples.

10. The Spiritual Works of Mercy include counseling the doubtful, instructing the ignorant, admonishing the sinner, comforting the sorrowful, forgiving injuries, bearing wrongs patiently, praying for the living and the dead.

    Read the following scriptures from the Bible:
    - Proverbs 19:20
    - 1 Corinthians 1:25
    - Psalm 32:1
    - Matthew 18:21–22
    - Hebrews 13:5
    - John 16:33
    - Psalm 141:5
    - Matthew 7:1–2
    - Exodus 14:14
    - Luke 9:51–59
    - Numbers 21:7
    - Luke 22:32
    - Hosea 4:6
    - Romans 2:20–24

    Find two scriptures to go with each spiritual work of mercy.

11. How is God's love linked from the Old Testament to the New Testament. Give examples from scripture.

12. Explain the three parts of the Holy Trinity. How are they alike? How are they different?

Study Guide D

13. Read John 14:16–17. What other names are used for God's spirit besides the Holy Spirit? How does this relate to you?

14. Explain the concept of hope and grace. Find this in scripture and document.

15. Read the poem "God Is Love." Circle the paragraph that moves you. Why does it stir your heart?

16. Read this poem again. Circle a few words that stand out to you. Write a prayer to Jesus, and include these words. Record the prayer in your journal to complete your personal book of prayers.

17. Play and sing your favorite songs or hymns about God's love for us.

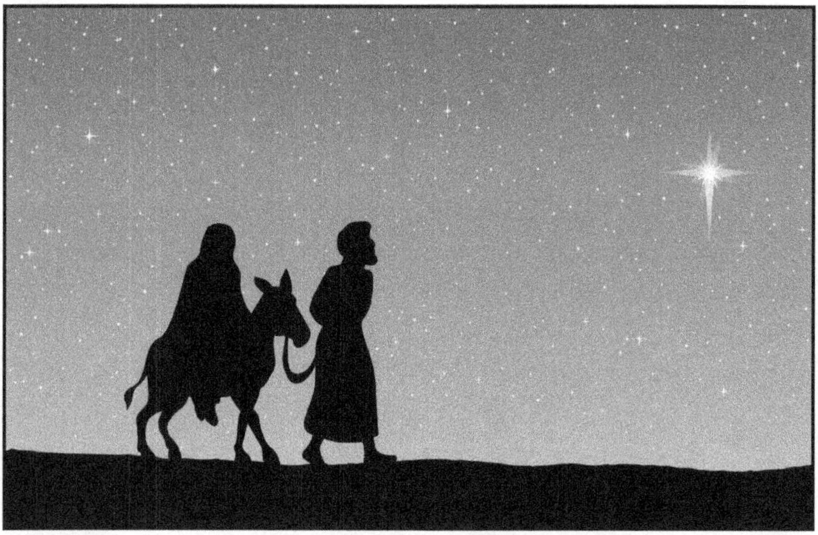

In Praise of Saint Joseph

Good Saint Joseph, guardian of the Most High
A soul who wandered but never asked why
An angel came down from heaven one night
And told him he would aid him on his flight.

The night was cold with no place to stay
The only bed was one of hay
To the glorious mother a child was born
Into the world He came and would receive much scorn.

His name was Jesus, a Savior for all
He was protected by Joseph, a mighty wall
An angel led them to safety one night
With Joseph always there during the flight.

Thanks to Saint Joseph, who was led by the dove
He protected our Savior, the God of love
So I praise you, O Lord, from your birth
You, the king of heaven and earth.

You came down from heaven to help us all
We who have sinned because of the fall
Through Your goodness, You gave us new life
To handle problems, grief, and strife.

Because of Your mercy and love for the lost
Another chance was given to all who were lost
We all confess and say from the heart
Forgive me, Lord, and thanks for a new start.

In Praise of Saint Joseph

Study Guide A

1. Are Mary and Joseph mentioned in the Old Testament of the Bible? If so, where in the Old Testament is Jesus mentioned? How are Jesus, Mary, and Joseph linked from the Old Testament to the New Testament? Document the scripture.

2. Joseph was called by God to protect Mary and her newborn son, Jesus. Joseph was visited three more times with instructions of what to do for his family as stated in Matthew chapter 2. What was Joseph instructed to do? Who gave him the directions? How was he to do this?

3. Read in the book of Matthew 1:20–24. What do you think would have happened if Joseph had followed his own understanding instead of trusting the message of the Lord revealed through the angel? Explain.

Study Guide B

4. Who is the "dove" that led Saint Joseph?

5. What can Saint Joseph teach us about trusting the Lord?

6. How are Saint Joseph and your father alike?

Study Guide C

7. Read in the book of John 1:12–13. What does scripture tell us about this child, Jesus, saving us?

8. In this poem, it states "another chance was given to all that were lost." Who are "the lost" ones? Why are they lost?

9. What can we learn from Proverbs 3:1–8 about our attitude toward Jesus?

Study Guide D

10. Why is Jesus called the King of Heaven and Earth?

11. Read this poem "In Praise of Saint Joseph." Circle the paragraph that stands out to you. Why does it move you?

12. Read this poem again. Circle a few words that stand out to you. Write a prayer to Jesus and include these words. Record the prayer in your journal to complete your personal book of prayers.

13. What can we do to keep the focus of Christmas on the birth of Jesus instead of material things of this world?

14. Play and sing your favorite songs or hymns about Saint Joseph.

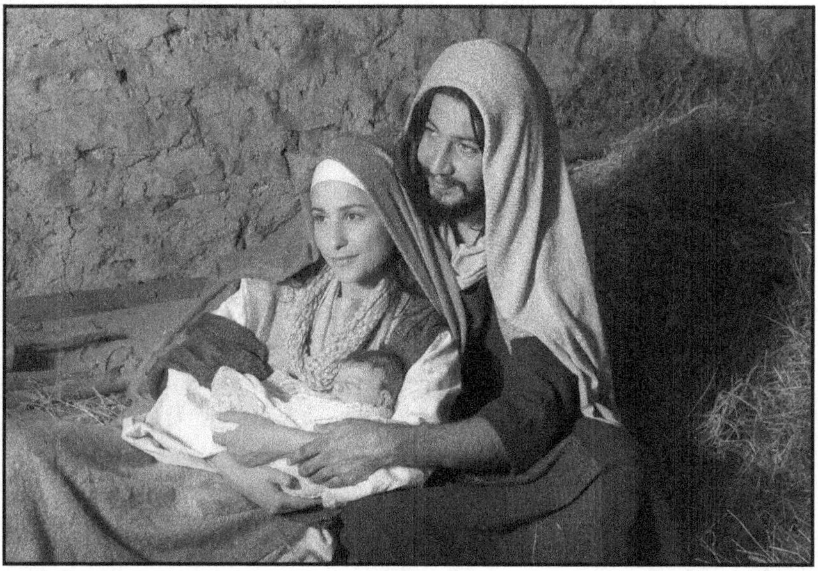

The Holy Family

Our Lord and Savior was brought to this earth
Through the Holy Spirit by a virgin birth.

Mary was chosen to bring Him here
His love for her was ever so dear.

She was placed on earth for a serious reason
To bring forth Jesus during the Christmas season.

Joseph was chosen to protect them here
Like a mighty warrior, they had no fear.

As Jesus grew in age, knowledge, and grace
He knew for sure this was His place.

The Holy Family

Study Guide A

1. In the beginning, the Word was God, and the Word became flesh. Who became flesh? Can you find this scripture in the book of John chapter 1 of the Bible?

2. How long has Jesus existed? Explain your answer.

3. How old was Jesus when He knew He was God's son?

4. How do you think Mary's parents felt when they learned that Mary was unmarried and expecting a baby? What had the prophet Isaiah predicted in the book of Isaiah chapter 7 of the Bible?

Study Guide B

5. How do you think the people of the village treated Mary when they found out she was pregnant and unmarried?

6. Read the book of Matthew 1:20–25. Why did Joseph change his mind about divorcing Mary?

7. Read Matthew 2:13–15. What did Joseph do to protect his family? What could his other choices have been?

8. How did Jesus know that the family was His place? How is this concept tied to the Old Testament?

Study Guide C

9. Mary is present at every important moment of her Son's life. She is there for the triumphs and the tragedies. Can

you name and discuss some of the triumphs and tragedies of Jesus's life and of your life?

10. Read Luke 2:39–52. This is the story of Jesus's growth. Compare His growth as a child to the growth of children today.

11. In Mary, we find the perfect example of a mother who encourages her son. Read in the book of John 2:1–2. How does she encourage Jesus at the wedding at Cana? How do you encourage your children?

12. Read Ephesians chapter 5. Explain how marriage and the family relate to the Holy Trinity from which all true love flows.

Study Guide D

13. How is this poem linked from the Old Testament to the New Testament? Find the scripture that proves your answer. Document the scripture.

14. Read the poem "The Holy Family." Circle your favorite stanza. Why is it your favorite?

15. Read the poem again, and circle several words that stand out to you. Write a prayer to Jesus, and include these words. Record the prayer in your journal to complete your personal book of prayers.

16. List and discuss at least five ways you can help your family become closer.

17. Play and sing your favorite songs or hymns about the Holy Family or your family.

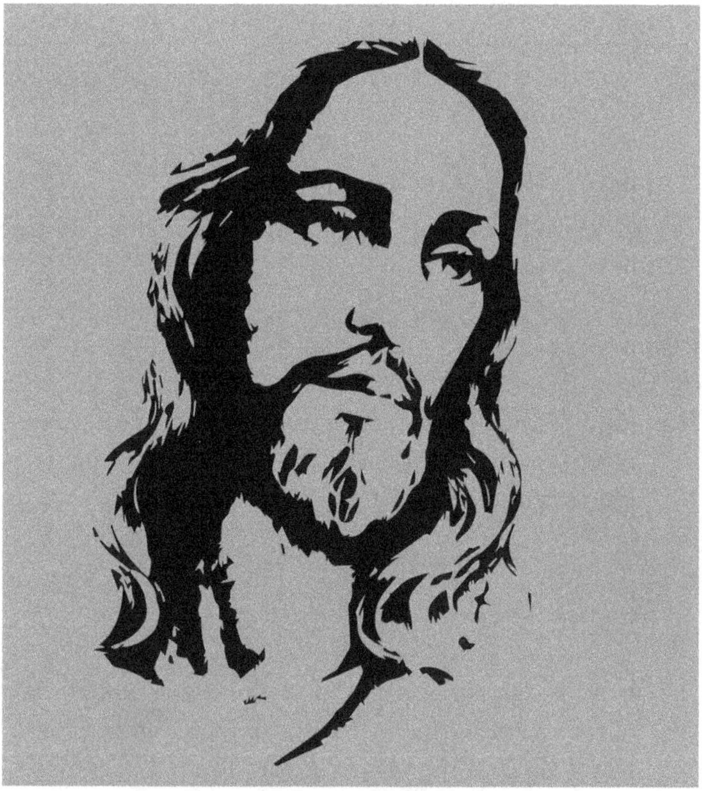

The Christ

Our Father in heaven sent His only Son
Down to earth for everyone.

His name was Jesus, a Savior for all
He came to save His people after the fall.

His love for mankind was ever so great
We knew then it was never too late.

His suffering on earth caused Him much pain
By allowing this, He knew we had much to gain.

His body and blood was then given to us
Because of this love we have someone to trust.

The Christ

Study Guide A

1. How long has Jesus existed? How do you know this?

2. Who is the "seed" God is referring to in the book of Genesis 1?

3. What is God's promise when He spoke to the serpent in the book of Genesis 3:14–15? How is this related to the "fall of mankind"?

Study Guide B

4. What did Simeon prophesy in the book of Luke 2:34–35?

5. Why did God choose to come as a baby and then die on the cross?

6. Did God continue to speak through the prophets? How did He do this? Who were the prophets to which He spoke?

Study Guide C

7. Christ suffered greatly in His life. Explain the ways you have suffered during your lifetime. How does this compare to Christ's suffering?

8. Compare your trust in Christ from ten years ago until now. Has it changed? If so, how has it changed?

9. What does receiving the body and blood of Jesus Christ mean to you?

Study Guide D

10. How is this poem linked from the Old Testament to the New Testament?

11. Read the poem "The Christ." Circle the paragraph in the poem that means the most to you. Why does it have a special meaning to you?

12. Add four more lines, or two more stanzas, to this poem. They can be added to the beginning, middle, or end of the poem. You can do it!

13. Read the poem again, and circle a few words that stand out to you. Write a prayer to Jesus, and include these words. Record the prayer in your journal to complete your personal book of prayers.

14. Play and sing your favorite songs or hymns about Christ.

Art Activity

To culminate this chapter, use your favorite art media to complete an original design that represents the poems in chapter 1, "The Birth of Jesus."

NOTES

NOTES

CHAPTER 2

The Teachings and Miracles of Jesus Christ

"I Am...a teacher and a miracle worker."

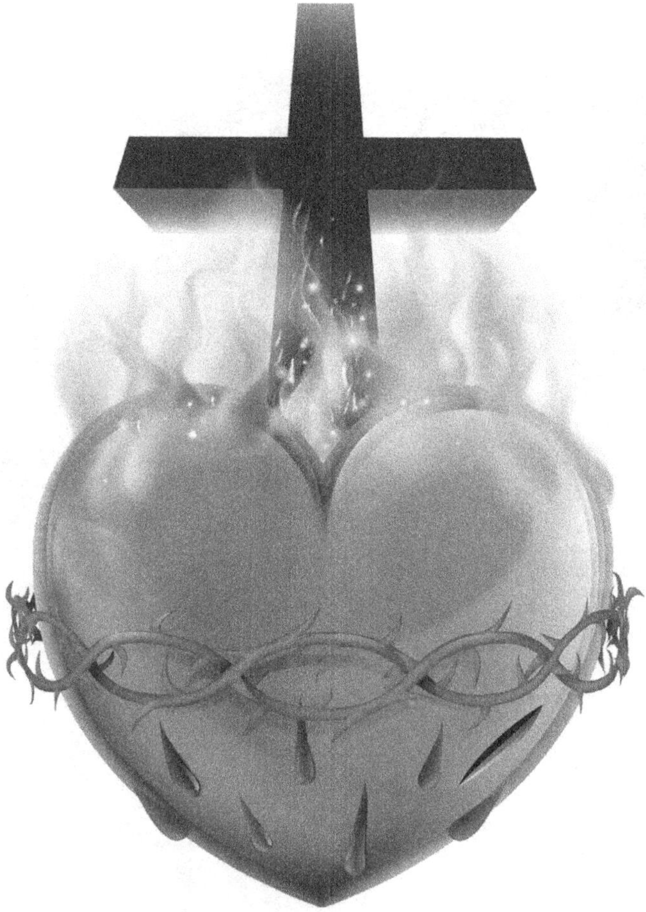

A Voice from the Heart

Oh heart of love, oh heart divine
What can I do to make you mine?

I look to the left, I look to the right
To get help from Him to fight the good fight.

Many times I'm down and all looks dim
But I know I can make it when I look at Him.

He gives me strength through His gentle love
And I will follow it through until I am with Him above.

My ups and downs are such a strife
But I know He is the only way to eternal life.

A Voice from the Heart

Study Guide A

1. How do you experience God's love?

2. God made us His through the sacrament of baptism. How do we make Him ours?

3. Why should I look to God for help?

4. What does the Sacred Heart of Jesus represent?

Study Guide B

5. The heart has always been a symbol of love. Why?

6. How does Jesus speak to us through the symbols of His sacred heart?

7. Find in scripture examples of "God's voice" in the Old Testament and the New Testament. How did He speak to people? Document the examples.

8. Read John 10:14–16. Why is Jesus's voice important in this scripture? How does this scripture relate to us?

Study Guide C

9. What scriptures assure you that God never leaves you?

10. During the difficult times in my life, how has God assured me that He was there for me to fight the good fight?

11. How have I handled my "ups and downs" differently now, as compared to five years ago? What made the difference?

12. Find five scriptures from the Bible that are meant to encourage us and give us hope when all looks dim. Document them.

Study Guide D

13. Read Psalm 95:7–11 and Hebrews 3:1–5. What do these scriptures mean to you?

14. What are some ways you can give assurance to other people?

15. Read the poem "A Voice from the Heart." Circle the paragraph that moves you. Why does it stir your heart?

16. Read the poem again. Circle a few words that stand out to you. Write a prayer to Jesus, and include these words. Record the prayer in your journal to complete your personal book of prayers.

17. Play and sing your favorite songs or hymns that tells us how God lifts us up.

Overthinking will steal your peace. Pray and leave it in **God's hands.**

God's Will

Our Lord and Savior gave us a new start
Uniting our wills with a gentle heart.

Uniting our wills is the only way
We must try and do this every day.

His love for us is ever so great
If you follow His will, it will never be too late.

His holy spirit dwells in us
To Jesus alone, who we can always trust.

So if we unite our wills in every way
We can always find in Him a place to stay.

God's Will

Study Guide A

1. Define discernment. Find three biblical scriptures that speak of discernment. Record them.

2. Think back to an earlier time in your life. What were the good decisions you made?

3. What were the factors you considered before making those decisions? What was your plan?

4. Recall an important decision you regret. Did you discern before you made the decision? Was God part of the process? What should you have done differently?

5. Have you ever encountered difficulties in your life when you were trying to live in God's will? What were they?

6. How did you overcome these difficulties?

Study Guide B

7. Did you have times during the last month when discernment was critical? What helped you make the right decision?

8. What are the benefits of living in God's will?

9. Read John 3:29–30. How is Jesus calling you to allow HIM to increase his presence in your life and asking you to decrease your dependency on yourself?

10. How well are you able to practice self-denial? List some examples.

11. In what ways do "uniting of our wills" form a direct correlation with Jesus's command to deny ourselves and pick up our cross?

Study Guide C

12. Read Luke 4:1–13 about the Temptation of Jesus in the Desert. What would have been the consequences if Jesus had followed the advice of Satan?

13. Read the following scriptures. What is the message in each scripture about God's will for you?

    - Jeremiah 29:11
    - 1 Thessalonians 4:3–6
    - Proverbs 3:6
    - Ephesians 5:15–21
    - Hebrews 10:36
    - Hebrews 13:20–21

14. How does obedience, prayer, and listening to the Holy Spirit help you live in God's will?

15. What does your daily prayer plan look like?

Study Guide D

16. How is God's will linked from the Old Testament to the New Testament?

17. Read the poem "God's Will." Circle the stanza or paragraph that attracts you. Why does this part of the poem stir your heart?

18. Read the poem again. Circle a few words that stand out to you. Write a prayer to Jesus, and include these words.

Record the prayer in your journal to complete your personal book of prayers.

19. Play and sing your favorite songs or hymns that guide you to God's will.

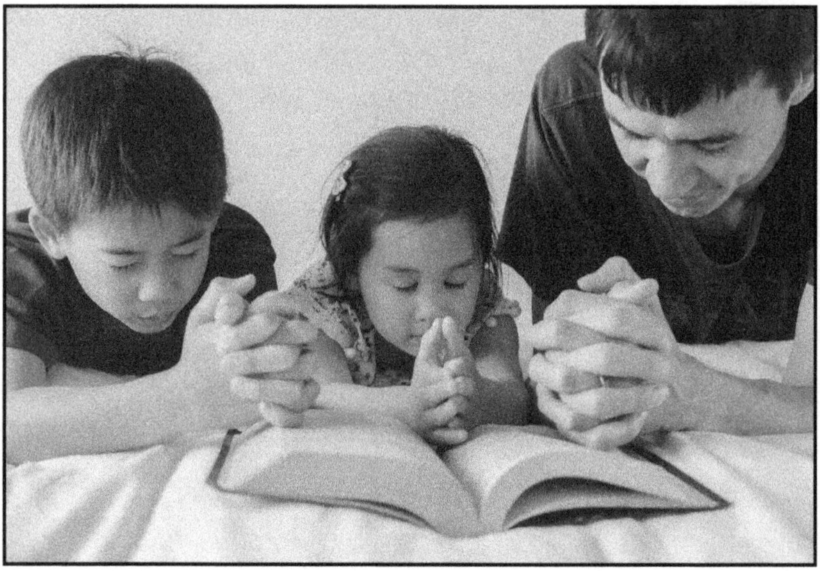

His Holy Word

You are my love, you are my life
Your holy word is like a double-edged knife.

In the depth of the Bible, a man must dwell
The parables are real just like show and tell.

When a man kneels down and prays hard
He will advance foot by foot, yard by yard.

If he spends some time reading His word
He can rest assure that all is heard.

So get down on your knees and ask for His grace
To meet Him one day face-to-face.

HIS HOLY WORD

Study Guide A

1. How does a "double-edged knife" relate to the Bible? What does that mean to you?

2. How has God revealed himself to you through scripture?

3. When have you encountered God through scripture? What was the scripture? Explain.

4. How does scripture comfort you? guide you? transform you?

Study Guide B

5. Describe in your own words the Holy Trinity. What is your basis for your answer?

6. Describe your plan for reading the Bible.

7. Find three scriptures in the Old Testament and three scriptures in the New Testament of the Bible that tell us how to show love to others. Please document.

Study Guide C

8. Find five scriptures in the New Testament where Jesus was teaching in parables. Describe each one. Please document.

9. Look at the scriptures you selected on love and the parables you selected in the New Testament. Do you feel they are *connected*? If so, how?

10. What are some things you can do in your everyday life to "turn your eyes from this world and follow him"? Can you find a scripture that supports your answer?

Study Guide D

11. Read the poem "His Holy Word." Circle the paragraph that means the most to you. Why does it move you?

12. Add two more stanzas or four lines to the poem. It can be at the beginning, middle, or end of the poem. You can do it!

13. Read the poem again. Circle several words that stand out to you. Now, write a prayer to Jesus, and include these words. Record the prayer in your personal book of prayers.

14. Play and sing your favorite songs or hymns about the Bible, the Word of God.

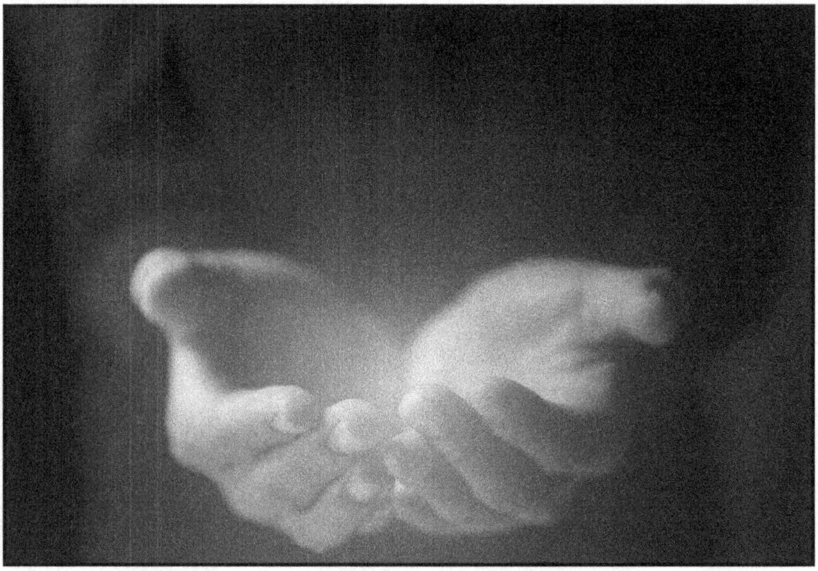

In the Palm of His Hand

Our Lord and Savior has a heart of gold
He is always with us young or old.

Love and mercy pour forth from His heart
Laying the foundation to give us a new start.

As we long to be with Him above
We can only get there through His mercy and love.

He has every one of us in the palm of His hand
Hoping each one of us gets to the Promised Land.

If we do what He says and follow His way
We can rest assure of an eternal home one day.

In the Palm of His Hand

Study Guide A

1. What does gold symbolize in Christianity?

2. God reminds us in four different ways that He has you in the palm of His hand. The ways are the following:

    - Immerse yourself instead of reminding yourself of promises.
    - Sing.
    - Look for evidence of grace all around you.
    - Surround yourself with positive people.
    How do you see each one of these ways in your life?

3. What does "in the palm of His hand" mean to you?

4. What does science say about the hand?

5. The meaning of *hand* in the Bible is meant to give authority in the form of guidance, instruction, and discipline. What does that look like in your life?

6. Read 2 Timothy 3:16–17 and James 1:5–7 in the Bible. How do these scriptures relate to guidance, instruction, and discipline?

Study Guide B

7. Why does scripture emphasize the right hand of God?

8. Read Psalms 110:1, 118:16; 1 Peter 3:22; and Acts 5:31. Explain each one as to how it relates to the right hand of God.

9. How do these scriptures relate to the hand of God moving in your life?

   1 Samuel 5:11   2 Chronicles 30:12–13
   Job 19:21, 27:11   Ecclesiastes 2:24–26, 9:1
   John 4:24

   Explain.

Study Guide C

10. When Jesus rode to Jerusalem on Palm Sunday, they laid palms out in the street to welcome Him. What do palms symbolize in the bible?

11. Why do Christians today wave palm leaves?

12. How does the Bible describe the Promised Land? What would it look like to you?

13. How are the Old Testament and the New Testament tied together in this poem?

Study Guide D

14. Read the poem "In the Palm of His Hand." Circle the paragraph that means the most to you. Why does it stir your heart?

15. Read the poem again. Circle a few words that stand out to you. Write a prayer to Jesus, and include these words. Record this prayer in your journal to complete your personal book of prayers.

16. Weave your Easter palms into crosses. If you are unsure how to do this, you can find the directions on YouTube. If

you have a priest, ask him to bless them. Put them in every room in your home and in your vehicles. What will this symbolize to you?

17. Play and sing your favorite songs or hymns about how God holds us in the palm of His hand. This also relates to support and protection.

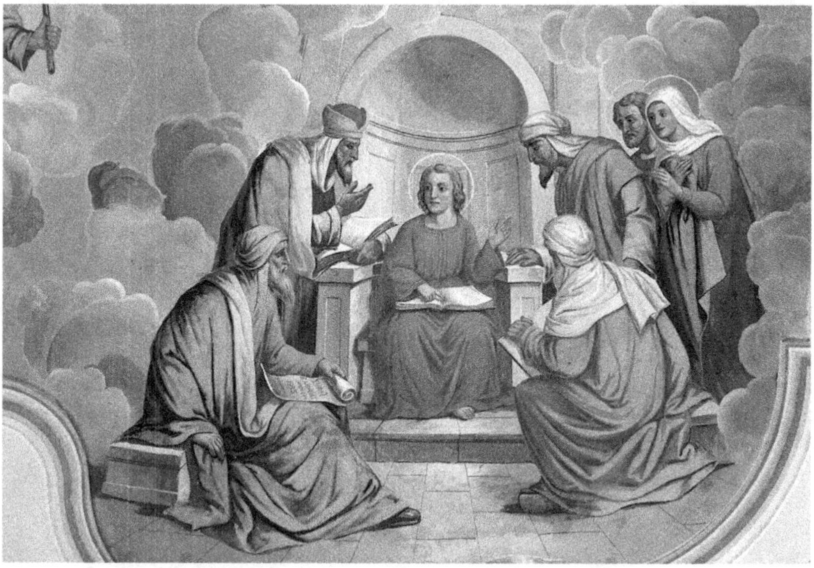

Jesus in the Temple

Jesus grew up and went to the temple
The message He gave was very simple.

The love of the Father and the Son
Comes together as three in one.

He spoke in parables and they understood
To love each other as best they could.

He remembered His Father and where He had been
Sharing love with His people to protect them from sin.

He died for us and rose from the dead
So turn your eyes from this world and follow Him instead.

Jesus in the Temple

Study Guide A

1. Why were Jesus, Mary, and Joseph visiting Jerusalem at this time of year?

2. Read in the book of Luke 2:41–52. What was Jesus doing with the priests and teachers for three days in the temple?

3. What were temples like during the time of Jesus? How would you describe the temple where Jesus was teaching?

4. What do you think the priests and teachers thought about the young Jesus and the knowledge He had at that young age?

5. Read Romans 8:9. How can we make our body a temple for the Holy Spirit? Explain.

Study Guide B

6. How are the Holy Trinity and an egg alike? Explain.

7. How did Jesus describe the Holy Trinity? Where can you find this in the Scripture?

8. Read in the book of Genesis chapter 18. Three men appeared to Abraham. Could this be one of the first ways of describing the Holy Trinity? How?

9. What does the Old Testament say about the Holy Trinity?

Study Guide C

10. What is a parable? What are some concepts Jesus taught through parables?

11. How does God and the holy Eucharist protect us from sin?

12. Why should we turn our eyes from this world and follow Him? What are the benefits to us?

13. In what ways do "uniting of our wills" form a direct correlation with Jesus's command to deny ourselves and pick up our cross?

14. We encounter Jesus in the temple through the Eucharist. How does the Eucharist help us to grow in love for one another? Where will you find this in scripture?

Study Guide D

15. Read in the Bible 1 Corinthians 6:19–20, 12:13; John 1:1–5, Luke 1:35, and Matthew 28:19 in the New Testament. How is the Holy Trinity described?

16. Fun activity! Draw a floor plan of the temple in which you think Jesus would have appeared. Where is it located? Design the rooms and figure the total square footage of the temple.

17. Read the poem "Jesus in the Temple." Circle the paragraph that stirs your heart. Why does it move you?

18. Read the poem again. Circle a few words that stand out to you. Write a prayer to Jesus, and include these words. Record the prayer in your journal to complete your personal book of prayers.

19. Play and sing your favorite songs or hymns about the Holy Trinity.

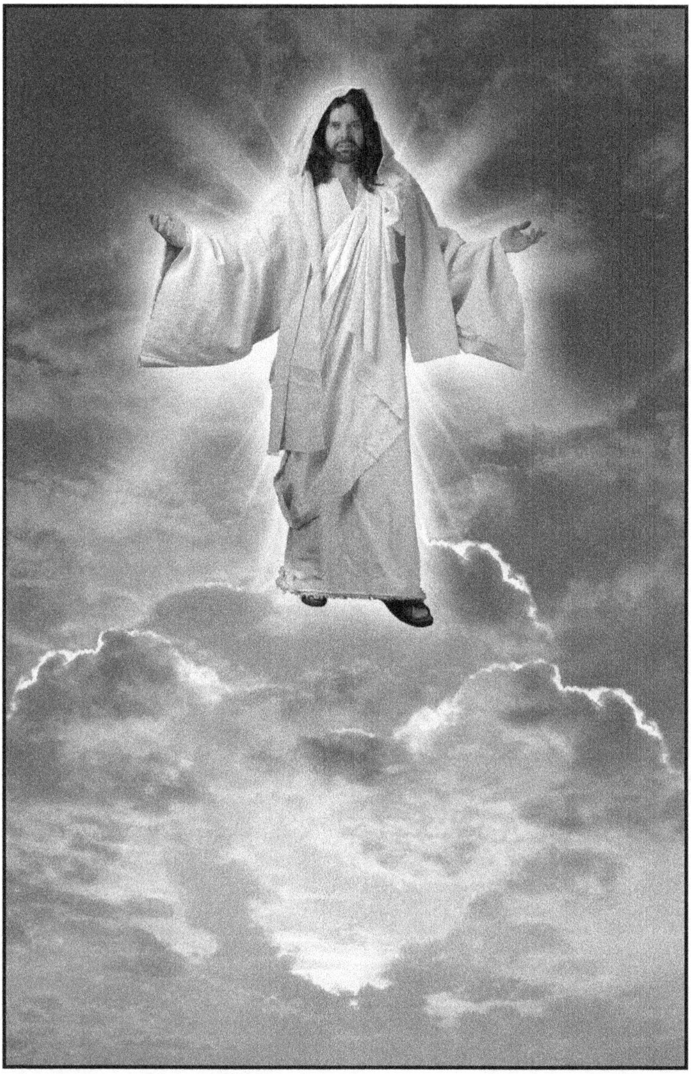

King of Heaven and Earth

I praise you, O Lord, from your birth
You are the king of heaven and earth.

You came down from heaven to help us all
Because we have sinned, on account of the fall.

Through your goodness You gave us new life
To handle problems that would cause us strife.

Because of your mercy and love of the cross
Another chance was given to all who were lost.

We all have to confess and say from the heart
Forgive us, Lord, and "thanks" for a new start.

King of Heaven and Earth

Study Guide A

1. Read in the book of Isaiah 53:6. What does Adam and Eve's sin have to do with you?

2. Is it comforting to know that Jesus's mercy overcomes all?

3. How does a new life in Christ help us to deal with anxiety and disappointment?

Study Guide B

4. Read Matthew 2:1–2. The magi, or three wise men, were believed to be men of high position in the area. How could they have known where the star they followed was leading them?

5. What did astrology and "following stars" mean to the people who lived during these times?

6. Before arriving in Bethlehem, the magi encountered King Herod. What was Herod's response when he learned they were seeking the one that was born "King of the Jews"? What scripture supports your answer?

7. The magi traveled thousands of miles to see the King of the Jews. When they found Jesus, how did they respond to Him? Compare their response then to how people in today's world would respond to Him.

Study Guide C

8. Read Matthew 9:13. How does Jesus's command to show mercy cause you to examine how you treat others?

9. In Paul's prayer to God in Ephesians 4:14–21, what is he telling us about proclaiming God as our King of heaven and earth?

10. Read Mark 10:45. What is God teaching us here?

11. Read Matthew 9:13. Why did Jesus choose to eat with sinners? What was His message?

Study Guide D

12. How and why does Jesus forgive us? Find this in scripture. Document.

13. Read the poem "King of Heaven and Earth." Circle the two-line stanza that moves you. Why does it move you?

14. Read the poem again, and circle a few words that stand out to you. Write a prayer to Jesus, and include those words. Record the prayer in your journal to complete your personal book of prayers.

15. Play and sing your favorite songs or hymns about Christ the King of heaven and earth.

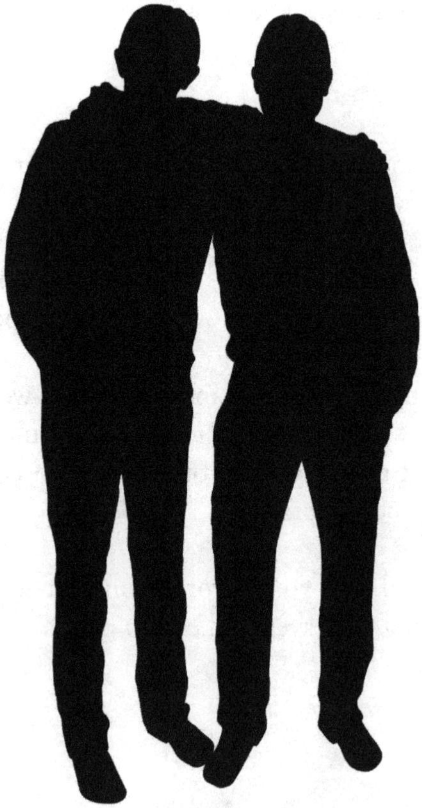

My Brother

As God reached down and took my brother
He gave me someone like no other.

His mother knew she had only one option
She prayed to God and gave him up for adoption.

Because He was a baby and encountered much strife
A family came along and gave him a new life.

He then grew with much wisdom and grace
His love for God grew at a rapid pace.

We knew there was love from the very first hug
It could only have happened by the Holy Spirit above.

My Brother

Study Guide A

1. What are some of the beautiful things that occur when someone gives up their baby for adoption?

2. The author of this poem is drawing attention to the possibility of choosing adoption over abortion. In today's world, adoption is often overlooked. Why do you think it is overlooked?

3. Do you think there is a stigma associated with adoption? Why or why not?

4. Modern-day adoption laws have changed. What is different about the adoptions of today compared to adoptions decades ago?

Study Guide B

5. Where is the concept of adoption found in the Old Testament and the New Testament? Please document the scripture.

6. What were the usual circumstances for adoption of a child during biblical times?

7. In what ways can we make the connection between the "poor widow" giving her whole livelihood and someone who gives their child up for adoption? Who receives "treasure" in adoption?

8. Read Romans 8:14–17. In the Roman culture, an adopted son or daughter inherited all rights and privileges of his/her new family. What are the privileges and responsibilities

afforded to you when you become part of the Christian family? Find this in scripture.

Study Guide C

9. Read Luke 23:38–43. How did Jesus show mercy to his brother on the cross at the Crucifixion? What was the response from the other brother? Explain how they were "adopted" into God's kingdom.

10. Though we were previously slaves to sin, how has Jesus adopted us into His kingdom? How can we claim full identity as His children?

11. As an adopted child of God, how do we share with Jesus all rights to God's resources?

Study Guide D

12. Read the poem "My Brother." Circle the stanza that means the most to you. Why does it move you?

13. Add two more stanzas or four lines to the poem. They can be added at the beginning, middle, or end of the poem.

14. Read the poem again. Circle several words that move you. Write a prayer to Jesus, and include those words. Record the prayer in your journal to complete your personal book of prayers.

15. Play and sing your favorite songs or hymns about adoption.

TEMPTATION...

Temptation

It looks like fun and all seems well
But all it is, is a fast pace to hell.

Satan will come and lead the way
Many will follow and go astray.

God can change your heart before the morning sun
From what you thought was a lot of fun.

So kneel down and pray and change direction
Making God in heaven your best selection.

Temptation

Study Guide A

1. What brings you happiness?

2. What does temptation mean to you?

3. Where did Satan come from? What were the circumstances?

4. Where is temptation first mentioned in the Bible? Can you find it in book, chapter, and verse?

5. What resulted from this temptation?

Study Guide B

6. Do both God and Satan tempt us? If so, how?

7. Read in the book of Matthew 4:1–11. How and where was Jesus tempted by the devil three times? How did Jesus respond?

8. Look back on your life. Can you recall times that "looked like fun" but was really a "fast pace to hell"? What were they? How did you respond?

9. Was this behavior encouraged? By whom?

Study Guide C

10. How does Satan come to us?

11. Read the books of Acts 5:3, 1 Peter 5:8, 1 Thessalonians 3:5, and 1 John 2:16. How does Satan tempt us in these scriptures?

12. Read in the book of Matthew chapter 4. What were the three temptations Jesus got from Satan? One was physical, one was emotional, and one was spiritual.

13. To "change our direction," we must resist Satan. Read James 4:7–8, Revelation 12:11, Ephesians 6:17–18, 1 Peter 4:7–11, and Luke 22:31–32. Explain how each scripture tells us how we can resist Satan and turn away from temptation.

14. How does the Eucharist help us resist temptation?

Study Guide D

15. Where is temptation found in the Old Testament and the New Testament? What links them together?

16. Read the poem "Temptation." Circle the stanza that means the most to you. Why does it move you?

17. Read the poem again. Circle several words that stand out to you. Write a prayer to Jesus, and include these words. Record this prayer in your personal book of prayers.

18. Play and sing your favorite songs or hymns about temptation.

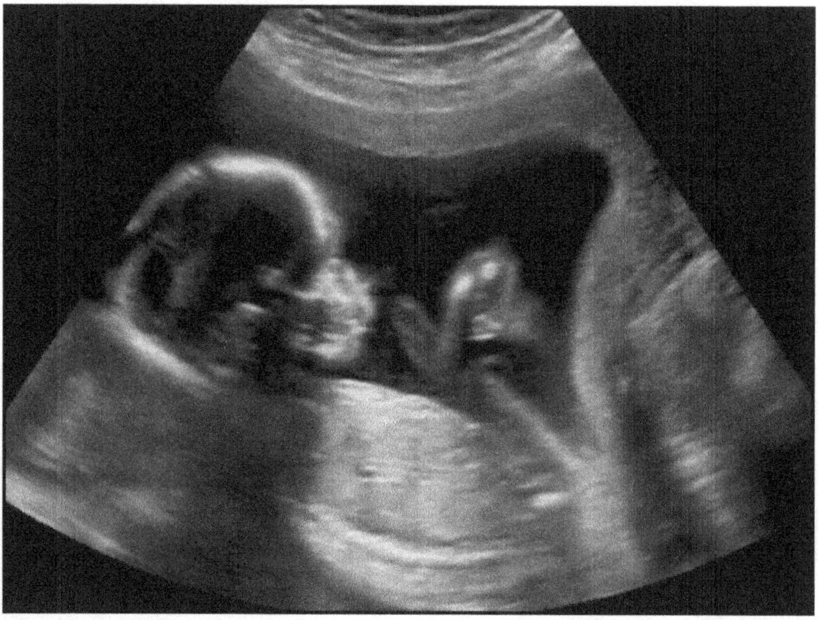

The Little One

I hear a voice, a voice from above
I wonder who and if there will be love.

As I sleep here in my mother's womb
I wonder if it will be my tomb.

My heart aches and sometimes I cry
Just from not knowing if I live or die!

I plead with my mom to have mercy on me
And I pray to God that she may see.

For I have a soul, I am full of life
And I don't wish to die by the blade of a knife.

I wish to be born and give glory to God
And woe the man struck by the rod.

For when it is said and all is done
He must pay, pay for the death of the little one!

The Little One

Study Guide A

1. This poem is a look at an unplanned pregnancy through the eyes of the unborn child. How does the author's assignment of personhood give us a new lens for which to see the unborn?

2. What importance did Jesus place on children? What importance does our modern-day culture place on children?

3. Read Matthew 19:13–15. Why did the disciples discourage the children from going to Jesus? What was Jesus's response?

Study Guide B

4. Where in scripture in the Old Testament and the New Testament can you find instances of women in a crisis pregnancy? What happened to them and their child?

5. Have you ever been discouraged from doing something when, really, you felt that discouragement was wrong? Explain.

6. Read Matthew 19:13–15. Think about the life of a new baby. What are the possibilities for him or her? How should you help?

Study Guide C

7. How could you help someone who is facing an unplanned pregnancy and is in crisis?

8. What resources are in your community to offer help to them?

9. Why is mental health support so critical for pregnant women who have made the choice for abortion?

Study Guide D

10. Read the poem "The Little One." Circle the stanza that means the most to you. Why does it move you?

11. Add two more stanzas or four lines to the poem. They may be added to the beginning, middle, or end of the poem.

12. Read the poem again, and circle a few words that stand out to you. Write a prayer to Jesus, and include those words. Record the prayer in your journal to complete your personal book of prayers.

13. Play and sing your favorite songs or hymns about the birth of a baby or lullabies for babies.

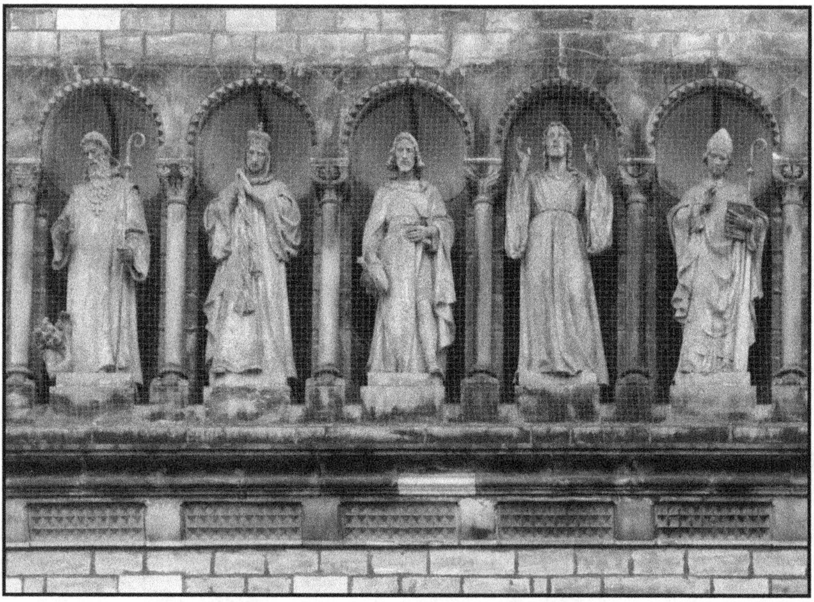

The Saints

God chose certain people from the earth
To imitate Him through Jesus's birth.

The saints grew in grace by suffering much pain
Their love for God gave them much to gain.

Since Jesus's birth they grew in love
Hoping one day to be with Him in heaven above.

We can pray and follow their way
Knowing it will lead us to God one day.

So if you kneel down and pray and ask for His grace
Like the saints, you will meet Him one day face-to-face.

The Saints

Study Guide A

1. All the saints have been called to pray for us. That is called an intercessory prayer. Are you comforted by the fact that we can invoke the saints in heaven to pray for us? Why or why not?

2. We are all called to be saints in heaven at the end of our lives. Right now, we should be saints in the making. How do you live each day of your life working toward sainthood?

3. Do you struggle with the challenge of being a saint in the making? Why or why not?

Study Guide B

4. Read the book of Matthew 9:9–13. Matthew was a wealthy tax collector. He put that aside to follow Jesus. He held a banquet. Not only was he physically hungry but he had a hunger of another kind. Can you explain this second type of hunger he had?

5. Have you ever had this kind of hunger stirred in you?

6. What do you think motivated Matthew's response to immediately follow Jesus?

Study Guide C

7. Read Luke 14:15–24. A man prepared a large dinner. He invited many people to the table. What excuses were given to the man by those not coming to the dinner? Why do you think they gave excuses?

8. Compare the excuses given by people for not coming to Jesus's table today or for not following Him to the excuses given in the parable.

9. Read Luke 5:27–32. What was it that made Jesus ask the men to follow Him? Why did Levi respond the way he did?

Study Guide D

10. Give examples in the Old Testament and the New Testament where people were asked to follow Jesus. Document the scripture.

11. List five of your favorite saints. Read about their lives. What are they known for?

12. Read the poem "The Saints." Circle the stanza that means the most to you? Why does it move you?

13. Read the poem again. Circle a few words that move you. Now write a prayer to Jesus, and include those words. Record your prayer in your journal to complete your personal book of prayers.

14. Play and sing your favorite songs or hymns about the saints.

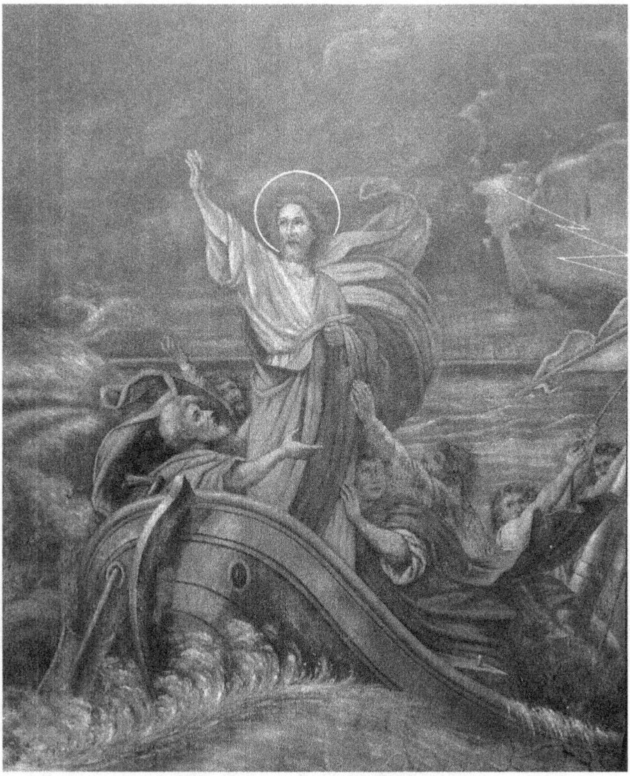

The Storm

Because of our sins along came a storm
Not so unusual but out of the norm.

God has a way of getting our attention
In too many ways even to mention.

His love for us is ever so great
For if we humble ourselves, it will never be too late.

We pray to Mary, our heavenly mother so dear
We can rest assure she is always near.

So we should ask God as we have before
Please have mercy on us and don't close the door.

The Storm

Study Guide A

1. Storms come in the form of physical, emotional, or spiritual storms. We all have them. When you encountered one of these storms, how did you respond to it?

2. In what ways has God shown you mercy through the storms in your life?

3. How does God use the storms in your life to help you draw nearer to Him? Give some examples from scripture.

4. What storms in your life have been a result of your sin? What could you have done differently?

5. What good things can come from the storms in your life?

Study Guide B

6. What are some of the storms our society has dealt with over the last twenty years? How did they affect you? How did you respond to them?

7. Recall three storms representing hard times in the Old Testament and three storms representing hard times in the New Testament. Remember all storms are not physical. Document the scripture.

8. Jesus even demonstrated His power over nature. Describe the miracle in the book of Matthew 8:23–27.

9. Read the geographical facts about the Sea of Galilee. What causes unexpected storms there?

Study Guide C

10. Jesus knew there would be a storm on the Sea of Galilee that day. Why do you think He took the disciples with Him?

11. Jesus's disciples were seasoned fishermen on this large lake. Why do you think the disciples panicked during the squall?

12. While the disciples were panicking, what was Jesus doing? What modern-day phrase could Jesus have used to reassure them?

13. How do you think Mark, Matthew, and Luke responded to the questions they asked each other after the storm? What was their plan? What was God teaching them?

14. In the book of Mark, it is said that "other boats were with Him." What do you think the onlookers in the other boats said when they saw what was happening? How did they justify their remarks?

Study Guide D

15. Who is with you in your boat during the storms in your life? How have they helped you?

16. Read the poem "The Storm." Circle your favorite paragraph. Why does it stir your heart?

17. Read the poem again. Circle a few words that stand out to you. Write a prayer to Jesus, and include these words. Record the prayer in your journal to complete your personal book of prayers.

18. Play and sing your favorite songs or hymns about storms, whether it be physical, emotional, or spiritual.

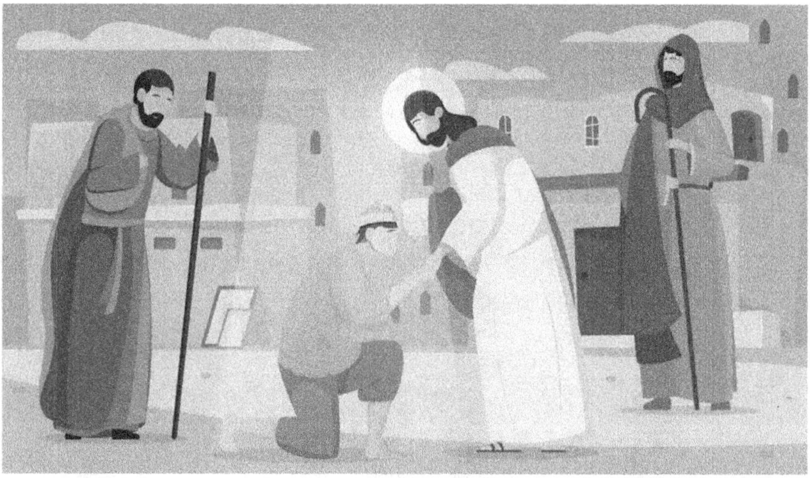

Miracles

Jesus worked many miracles while he walked around
Staying at homes of friends while in town.

He worked many miracles while standing at the door
People kept seeking him, wanting to see more.

They then surrounded him and wanted him to stay
But he knew it was time for him to get away.

He then went to the desert knowing it was best
It was a place for him to pray and rest.

For forty days and forty nights
He spent this time after this flight.

He fasted and spent his time praying
Hoping that people could understand what he was saying.

MIRACLES

The Bible records Jesus's miracles in all four gospels. Not only did Jesus work many miracles as "HE walked around town" but people "kept seeking HIM" like the friends of the paralytic man recorded in Matthew 9:2–8, Mark 2:3–12, and Luke 5:18–20.

Study Guide A

1. Where did Jesus's encounter with the paralytic man take place? What would that have looked like to you?

2. Who brought the paralytic man to Jesus? Describe the obstacles, if any, faced by these people.

3. In Luke 5:17–26, how did the people respond to the events they witnessed when the paralyzed man was lowered into the house from the roof?

4. Jesus's healing of the paralytic accomplished two purposes. What are they? Explain.

Study Guide B

5. Why is the fish a symbol of Christianity? When was this symbol first used?

6. Describe the miracle of the loaves and fishes (Luke:9 12–17). There was food left over. What does this mean to you?

7. Fun activity! How many baskets of bread were left after the five thousand ate? How many baskets did Jesus start with? About how many loaves were there in each basket?

8. Describe the miracle of the blind man at Bethsaida (Mark 8:23–27). How are these miracles alike? How are they different?

Study Guide C

9. Jesus spent forty days in the desert praying. How does this time in the desert illustrate Jesus's teachings of the necessity of prayer?

10. Read Matthew 4:1–11 describing Jesus's forty days in the desert. Describe the temptation Jesus faced while in the desert. What miracles do you observe in this passage?

11. How is Jesus's practice of fasting and prayer reflected in our own spiritual life?

12. Are you always aware of miracles in your own prayer life? Why or why not?

Study Guide D

13. Find and document a few miracles found in the Old Testament and a few from the New Testament. How are they connected? Do not use those mentioned in this study guide.

14. Read the poem "Miracles." Circle the stanza or paragraph that moves you. Why does it stir your heart?

15. Read the poem again. Circle a few words that stand out to you. Write a prayer to Jesus, and include these words. Record the prayer in your journal to complete your personal book of prayers.

16. Play and sing your favorite songs or hymns about miracles.

Art Activity

To culminate this chapter, use your favorite art media to create an original work of art that represents the poems in chapter 2, "The Teachings and Miracles of Christ."

Notes

Notes

CHAPTER 3

The Holy Eucharist

"*I Am*...the Holy Trinity present in the Eucharist."

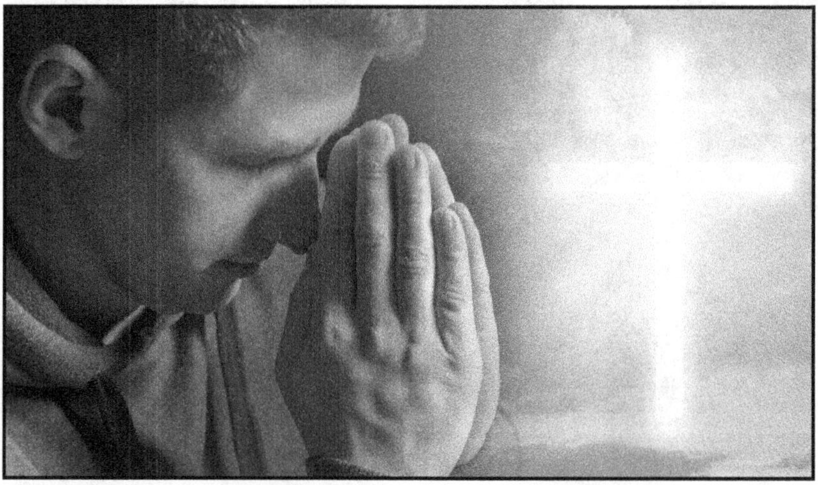

A Prayer for Priests

O Holy God, Lord of hosts
Bless our priests with the Holy Ghost.

Give them graces to come through the day
Shower them with love, for this we pray.

You placed them on earth to imitate You
Many were called but You chose only a few.

You gave them power to change bread and wine
Into Your body and blood, eternally divine.

So protect them from the evil one
And stay by their side until Your work is done.

A Prayer for Priests

Study Guide A

1. What are some of the sacrifices a man must make when choosing to become a priest?

2. Why do you think a man would still choose the priesthood over the sacrifices that must be made?

3. What was the role of the priests in the Old Testament and their roles in the New Testament? How are they alike? How are they different? Document a scripture to validate your answers.

Study Guide B

4. Why should we pray for priests?

5. How can we show them support?

6. What is the priest's role in the consecration of the mass?

7. What is the role of the priest when hearing confessions?

8. What is the seal of confession in the Catholic Church? What does that mean to you?

Study Guide C

9. How can God protect priests and us from the evil one?

10. In an average year, three thousand men enter the seminary. Only 430 to 470 complete their training for the priesthood. What is the percentage of success of priests achieving their goal for the priesthood?

11. What are the greatest struggles that priests have in today's world?

Study Guide D

12. How are priests of Catholic churches and pastors of Protestant churches alike? How are they different?

13. Read the poem "A Prayer for Priests." Circle the paragraph that stirs your heart. Why does it move you?

14. Read the poem again. Circle a few words that stand out to you. Write a prayer to Jesus, and include these words. Record your prayer in your journal to complete your personal book of prayers.

15. What else would you like to know about the life of a priest?

16. Play and sing your favorite songs or hymns about priests.

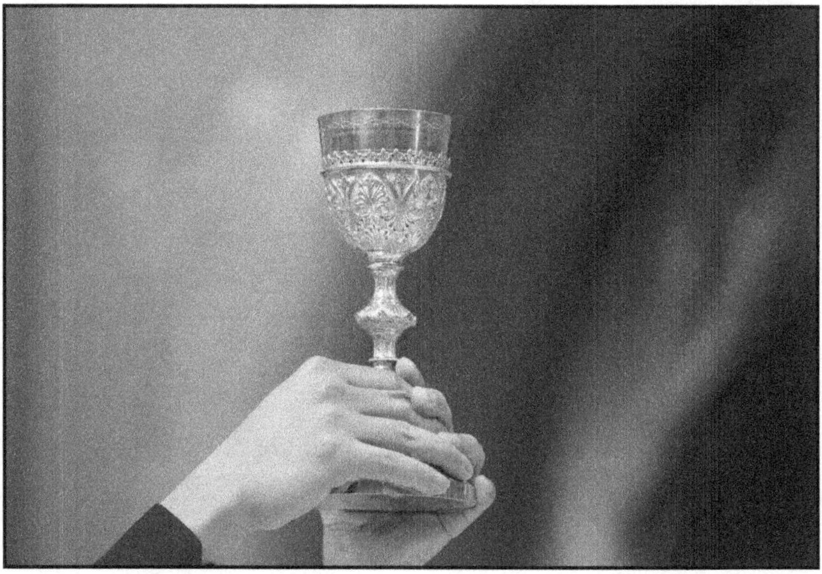

Consecration Prayer

O Jesus, mingle my sins in the chalice of your blood
Cleanse my soul, my heart, and my mind
So I may be worthy to receive
The gifts of the Holy Spirit.

Pope, Saint John Paul II, pray for us.

Consecration Prayer

Study Guide A

1. What is the meaning of *consecration*?

2. What do these five scriptures tell us about consecration: Joshua 3:5, 1 Corinthians 7:1–6, Psalm 51:2–7, 2 Samuel 12:20–23, and Colossians 3:5–14?

3. What does it mean to be consecrated by the Holy Spirit?

4. What are some sacrifices you can make in your life to turn your life over to that consecration?

Study Guide B

5. What does "mingle my sins in the chalice of your blood" mean to you?

6. Through what sacrament are we afforded the privilege to cleanse our soul, our heart, and our mind? What does this mean to you?

7. Do you allow God to be God in your life? Why? Why not?

8. Do you allow God to forgive you of your sins? Why? Why not?

9. Do you allow God to carry away your guilt? Why? Why not?

Study Guide C

10. What are the three parts of the liturgy of the Eucharist? Describe each one.

11. How are bread and wine turned into the body and blood of Jesus Christ?

12. Bells are rung during the consecration. What does this part of the mass mean? What is the word used for describing the changing of bread and wine into the body and blood of Jesus Christ?

13. What is the priest's role in turning the bread and wine into the body and blood of Christ?

Study Guide D

14. Why does the priest break off a piece of the eucharist and put it in the chalice during the consecration?

15. Over the centuries, many priests have doubted that the host was really the body and blood of Christ. What did God allow to happen to convince them?

16. Read the "Consecration Prayer." Circle a few words that stand out to you. Write a prayer to Jesus, and include these words. Record the prayer in your journal to complete your personal book of prayers.

17. In the Catholic church, what songs are appropriate to be sung during the consecration?

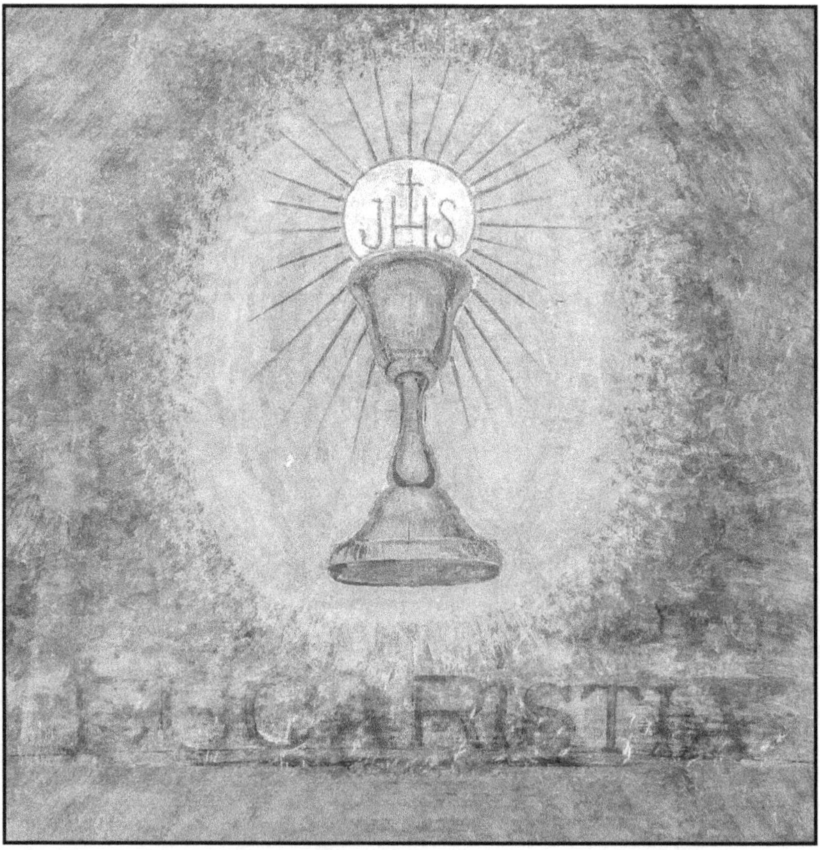
JHS
EUCARISTIA

The Holy Eucharist

God, our Father, in heaven above
Sent His Son down with the greatest gift of love.

It is the Holy Eucharist, a gift for all
The greatest source of grace after the fall.

His body is real food, His blood is real drink
The changes take place before the eye can blink.

His body and blood the best source of good health
Better than all things on earth and all its' wealth.

So when in His presence all knees must bend
Because He will be with us until the very end.

The Holy Eucharist

Study Guide A

1. What does the word *eucharist* mean?

2. The Old Testament cites the coming of the Eucharist in three places:

   - Melchizedek—Genesis 14
   - The original Passover—Exodus 12
   - Manna for the Israelites—Exodus 16 and Numbers 11:1–9

   Describe each one.

3. Five scripture readings mention the Holy Eucharist in the New Testament. Find the verses that mention the Holy Eucharist in each of these scripture readings. Document them.

   - Matthew 26
   - Luke 22
   - John 6
   - 1 Corinthians 11
   - Acts 2

4. What does each of the above scriptures mean to you?

Study Guide B

5. Define *grace*. What is our greatest source of grace?

6. How does grace relate to the Holy Eucharist?

7. What is a sacrament? Why is the Holy Eucharist the most important of all sacraments?

8. How is the Holy Eucharist the greatest gift of love?

Study Guide C

9. Why is the Holy Eucharist called the host? What are the hosts we receive at communion?

10. What happens to your body when you fill up on popcorn? Does the spiritual "junk food" we eat have any nutritional value? How does this affect us?

11. What kind of spiritual nourishment should we be seeking? Why is this nourishment called "food for the journey"?

12. How does the Holy Eucharist help us?

13. What does science say about the host becoming the flesh and blood of Jesus Christ? Has this been scientifically proven? What were the results?

Study Guide D

14. What are the gifts from God's son that are included in the Holy Eucharist?

15. What is the symbolism, meaning, and significance of the Last Supper?

16. In 1 Corinthians 11:23–33, St. Paul gives a warning about receiving the body and blood of Christ unworthily. How does this poem help our understanding of why it is important to be in a state of grace when receiving holy communion?

17. Read the poem "The Holy Eucharist." Circle a few words that stand out to you. Write a prayer to our Lord, and

include these words. Record the prayer in your journal to complete your personal book of prayers.

18. Play and sing your favorite songs or hymns about the Eucharist.

Art Activity

To culminate this chapter, use your favorite art media to complete an original design that represents the poems in chapter 3, "The Holy Eucharist."

NOTES

NOTES

CHAPTER 4

The Crucifixion

"I Am...the crucified Savior."

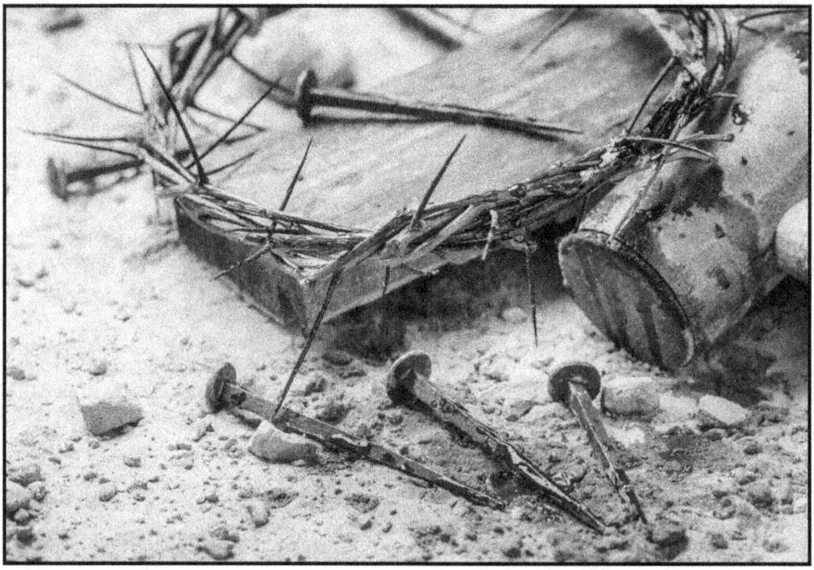

Heart-to-Heart

O Sacrament most Holy, O Sacrament Divine
Open your heart and make me thine.

Your body was nailed and fastened to the cross
You did all of this for me who was lost.

Your heart was pierced and your blood poured out
By letting this happen I was given a new route.

The road to heaven was opened once more
It would be hard for the rich, but easy for the poor.

The humble were lifted, the proud were down cast
If I wish to be first, I must be last.

So to meet Him in heaven on that great day
I must do as He does and follow His way.

Heart-to-Heart

Study Guide A

1. What is a sacrament? How do you become closer to God through the sacraments?

2. Why did Jesus suffer for us?

3. What facts can you find regarding the size of nails and dimensions of the cross? How much would you estimate that the cross of Jesus weighed?

4. Where was Jesus pierced by the sword of the Roman soldier?

Study Guide B

5. Read in the book of John chapter 20. One of the apostles had doubts about Jesus's wounds. Who was that apostle?

6. What did Thomas want as proof? What nickname was given to him? What is the scripture verse where it can be documented?

7. Read in the book of Matthew chapter 19. Find the verse that says it is more difficult for a rich man to get to heaven. What does this verse mean to you?

8. Scripture says you must humble yourself and think of others first. Can you find this verse in the books of Matthew and James? Document them.

9. What have you done in your life to put others first?

Study Guide C

10. If you want to go to heaven, you must follow Jesus. Why?

11. What does the author of this poem mean when he says "on that great day"?

12. Read in the Old Testament Psalm 16, Jeremiah 29, and 1 Chronicles 16. Find the verse or verses in each chapter that speak of following God's way. Document them.

13. Jesus says in John 14:6, "I am the way, and the truth, and the life; no one comes to the Father but through me." Is there more than one way to God? Explain.

Study Guide D

14. Read the poem "Heart to Heart." Add two more stanzas or four more lines to the poem. They may be added at the beginning, middle, or end of the poem. You can do it!

15. Read the poem "Heart to Heart." Choose five or six words that stand out to you. Write your own prayer to Jesus, and include these words in your prayer. Record the prayer in your journal to complete your personal book of prayers.

16. Play and sing your favorite songs or hymns about seeking the heart of Jesus.

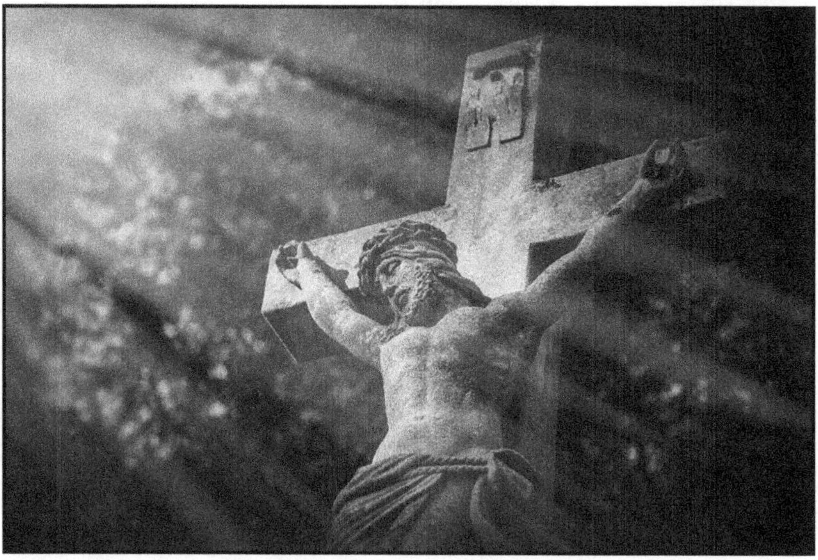

I Thirst

One of Christ's last words on the cross
Were directed to us who were lost.

So as the words came to our mind
We know for sure they were divine.

These two words were directed to us
Giving us hope and someone to trust.

We hope these words would quench His thirst
Begging for us to put Him first.

So as we try and struggle to the end
We know for sure we are going to win.

I Thirst

Study Guide A

1. What are the twelve stations of the cross? Describe them. Name some significant events that happened along the way.

2. Describe a crucifixion.

3. Gall is mentioned as one of the ingredients of the sour wine drink given to Christ on the cross. What is gall? What is myrrh? Why were these two ingredients mixed to form a drink that was offered to Jesus while He was on the cross?

4. What was a hyssop branch used for during the time of Jesus?

5. How long was Jesus on the cross until He died?

Study Guide B

6. What were Christ's last words as He was dying on the cross? What do these words mean to you?

7. Why does Jesus's last words give us hope?

8. Recall a time when you were extremely thirsty. What did that thirst feel like to you?

9. Can you recall a time in your life when you felt Jesus thirsted for you?

10. What do you thirst for in your physical life? In your spiritual life?

Study Guide C

11. What is Jesus thirsting for in my life today and in the world in which we live?

12. When you put Jesus first in your life, things seem to go better. Why?

13. What do you think the author of this poem was referring to when he said we will "win"?

14. What are five things you could do to reduce struggles in your everyday life?

Study Guide D

15. Read the poem twice. Circle the stanza that means the most to you. Why does it move you?

16. Read the poem again. Circle the words that stand out to you. Write a prayer to Jesus, and include those words. Record the prayer in your journal to complete your personal book of prayers.

17. Play and sing your favorite songs or hymns about thirst.

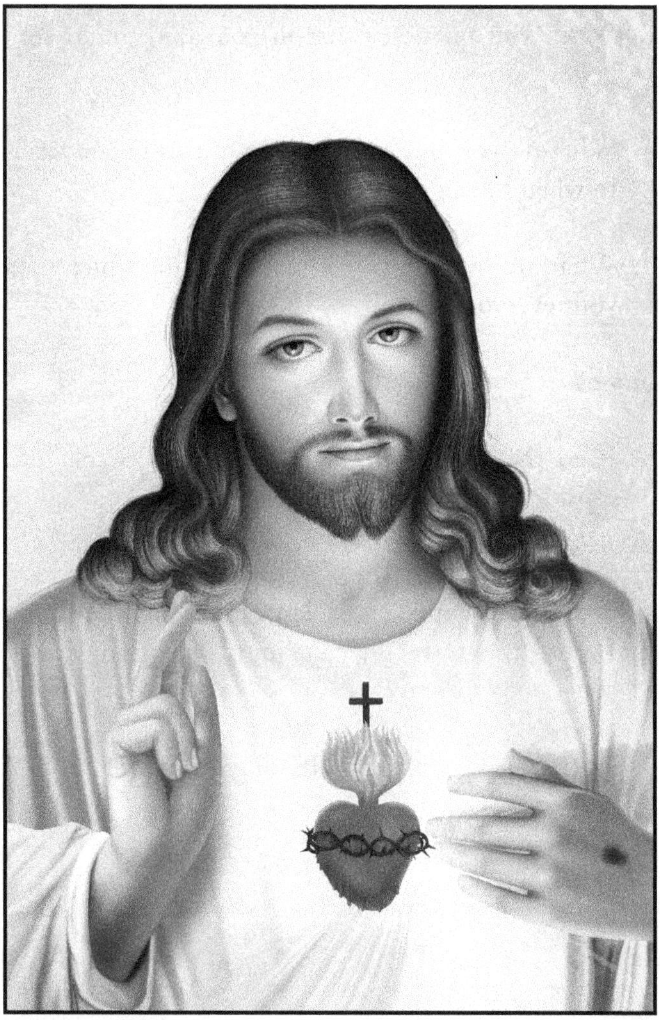

LOVE

The most Sacred Heart, our Lord above
Appeared to Saint Margaret Mary asking for love.

He opened His arms and showed His heart
He willingly forgave giving us a new start.

The thorns in His heart hurt Him so much
All He wants from us is to keep in touch.

The rays from His heart spread far and wide
He loves us so much He is bursting inside.

The wound in His side was really sore
The blood and water opened the door.

The cross above is a sign of our fate
Without the cross, it would have been too late.

If we heed these signs and symbols of love
One day we will be with Him in heaven above.

LOVE

Study Guide A

1. Who was Saint Margaret Mary? Where did the Lord appear to her?

2. What is agape love? How can we view the cross as a symbol of "agape love"?

3. Why did we need Jesus to give His life for us?

4. Why did Jesus so willingly forgive us? Find three scriptures in the Old Testament and three scriptures in the New Testament that speak of forgiveness. Document the scriptures.

Study Guide B

5. Jesus suffered for our sins. What does that mean to you?

6. The Sacred Heart of Jesus is a central theme throughout the Bible. It is a reference to Christ himself, not to the anatomy of the human body. The Sacred Heart represents the total person of Jesus.

    - What does the crown of thorns around the Sacred Heart symbolize?

    - What do the thorns around the Sacred Heart represent?

    - What does the flame that engulfs the Sacred Heart symbolize? What is the purpose of the fire?

    - What is the significance of the cross above the Sacred Heart?

- What is the meaning of the small gash on the Sacred Heart? What is it called?

7. How can the signs and symbols of the Sacred Heart guide you in your own life?

8. Find a picture of the Divine Mercy. What do the red rays and the pale rays mean?

Study Guide C

9. Why does the blood and water "open the door"? What does that mean to you?

10. What meaning does the symbolic cross have in this poem?

11. Find scriptures in the books of Matthew, Mark, Luke, and John that speak of someone with a "burden to carry" or a "cross to bear." Document the scriptures. What cross do you carry to show your love for someone?

12. Read the poem "Love." Circle the two-line stanza that means the most to you. Why does it stir your heart?

Study Guide D

13. Read the poem again. Circle a few words that stand out to you. Write a prayer to Jesus and include these words. Record the prayer in your journal to complete your personal book of prayers.

14. Add two more questions to this study guide.

15. Play and sing your favorite songs or hymns about the Sacred Heart of Jesus.

it is finished

It Is Finished

Our Lord and Savior was nailed to the cross
For all of us sinners and those who were lost.

He looked down on each of us
Giving us hope and someone to trust.

His heart was grieved and He hurt so much
Hoping one day we would keep in touch.

His side was pierced with a lance
His pain was terrible but it gave us another chance.

His arms stretched out and His hands were nailed
His feet were pierced and I know He yelled.

He then died on the cross after He cried out
"It is finished," thus giving us a new route.

It Is Finished

Study Guide A

1. How would you define people that are "lost"? Read in Luke 19:10. How did Jesus save the lost?

2. Read Luke 15:3–31. What are the three parables that mention the "lost"?

3. Find three scriptures in the Old Testament and three scriptures in the New Testament that tell us that we should pray. Document the scriptures.

4. Why is Jesus hurt when we fail to pray?

5. What happened in the book of Genesis chapter 22 that foretold that the Crucifixion would come much later? How are the two events related?

Study Guide B

6. Why did Jesus decline sour wine on the cross then later changed His mind and would accept it?

7. What exactly is a hyssop branch? Read in the book of John 19:29. What was the significance of the hyssop branch during the Crucifixion?

8. How were the hands and feet nailed to the cross during the Crucifixion?

9. Read the book of Isaiah 53:4–6. How does this scripture relate to the Crucifixion?

Study Guide C

10. Which of Jesus's last words resonate with you and why?

11. What is the implication of "It Is Finished"? Why did Jesus feel He had to say this before He died?

12. In this poem, there are five very important messages that relate to Jesus's sacrifices on the cross. What are they?

13. How does Christ dying on the cross and rising from the dead help us? Find this in scripture to validate your answer.

14. What has greater significance in your life: Christ crucified or Christ risen? Why?

Study Guide D

15. Read in John 19:30. What was Jesus's final act after announcing "it is finished"?

16. What system or sacrament in the Catholic church allows us to be forgiven or atoned for our sins?

17. Read the poem "It Is Finished." Circle a few words that stand out to you. Write a prayer to Jesus, and include these words. Record the prayer in your journal to complete your personal book of prayers.

18. Fun activity. Plan some Easter snacks during the Holy Week to celebrate Easter:

    - Crown of thorns: Ritz crackers spread with peanut butter. Add small broken pieces of pretzels to represent the thorns.

- Crosses: straight pretzels crossed. Add peanut butter where they cross one another to help hold them together.
- Stuffed olives: Jesus ascended from the Mount of Olives. Remove the pimento from the olive, and you have an "empty" tomb.
- Dark chocolate chips: represent the darkness of sin.
- Red candies such as red M&M's or cut Twizzlers strips to represent the blood of Jesus shed for us.
- Goldfish crackers: represent fish and bread that was considered staple food during the time of Jesus.
- Boiled eggs: slice and open them up. Remove the yolk. The tomb is empty. Use the yolks and mix with mayonnaise to make a mixture to stuff the eggs.

Have an Easter egg hunt. If you stuff the plastic eggs, leave one empty. When this empty egg is found, we know that Jesus has risen!

19. Play and sing your favorite songs or hymns related to "It Is Finished."

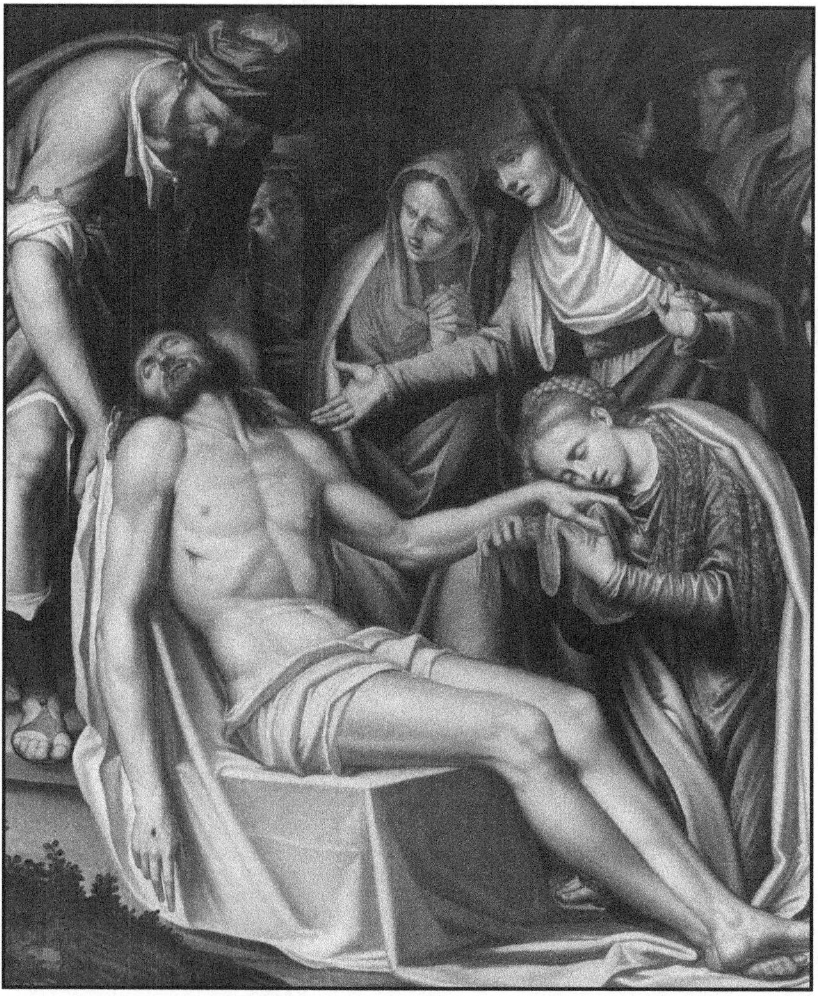

A Holy Death

A holy death, a gift for all
Made possible by Christ after the fall.

He came upon earth to give us new life
To relieve us from suffering and things that cause strife.

Though our trials and tribulations can lead us astray
He gives us graces to find our way.

As we close our eyes and go to sleep
He watches over us as He would His sheep.

He will then lead us to His father in heaven above
As we fly to Him on the wings of a dove.

A Holy Death

Study Guide A

1. How does Christ's death on the cross relate to the deaths of human beings?

2. How does Christ, talking to His Father at the time of crucifixion, relate to the experience of a family losing a loved one?

3. British author John Milton wrote, "Death is the golden key that opens the palace of eternity." What does this quote mean to you?

Study Guide B

4. What does a holy death mean to you? Why would a person desire a holy death?

5. What actions, or inactions, could impact the holiness of a person's death?

6. Read one or two of the following Bible chapters: Revelation 21, Psalm 34, Psalm 147, or John 14. Find the verses that give comfort to the dying.

Study Guide C

7. In biblical times, if people did not die of natural causes, what was usually their cause of death?

8. Read John 3:16. What is God's promise to those who believe in Jesus Christ as their Savior and Lord?

9. What trials and tribulations in your life lead you away from Christ?

Study Guide D

10. How does this poem relate to the childhood prayer "Now I Lay Me Down to Sleep"?

11. Why did the author use the "wings of a dove" in the poem instead of the stronger phrase "wings of an eagle"?

12. Read the poem "A Holy Death." Select your favorite stanza. Why does it move you?

13. Read the poem again. Circle a few words that stand out to you. Write a prayer to Jesus, and use these words. Record the prayer in your journal to complete your personal book of prayers.

14. Play and sing your favorite songs or hymns about a holy death.

Art Activity

To culminate this chapter, use your favorite art media to complete an original design that pulls together all the poems in chapter 4, "The Crucifixion."

NOTES

NOTES

CHAPTER 5

Tribute to the Blessed Mother and Her Grief

"**I Am**...Jesus, the son of Mary."

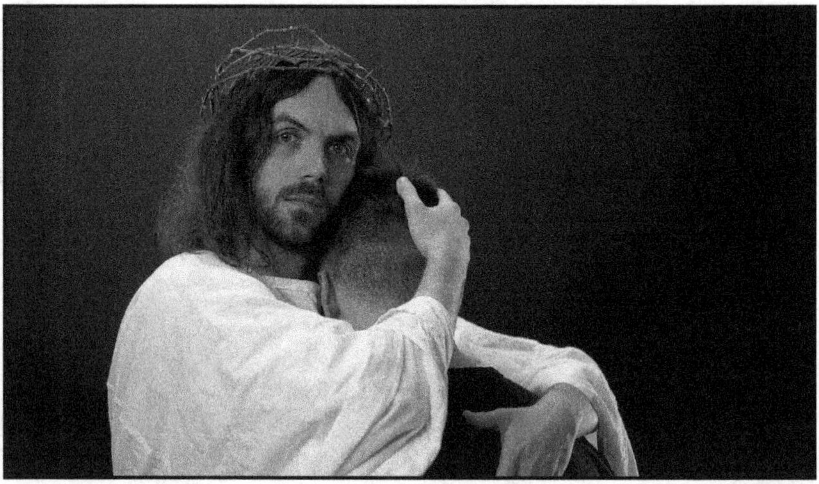

GRIEF

My soul is sad beyond belief
As I lay here crying in my grief.

I lost the person, my one true love
But I can look to heaven and see them above.

My heart aches and sometimes I cry
But I know someday I, too, must die.

Our time is short, we do our best
I know with God's help we can accomplish the rest.

He gives us graces throughout the day
Helping each other along the way.

As I close out His words of love
You will be with Me in heaven above.

Grief

Study Guide A

1. How have you experienced grief in your life?

2. How has a grief experience changed your life?

3. Can you identify ways that grief has strengthened your faith?

4. When you think about eternity in heaven, how can this help you if you are grieving?

Study Guide B

5. Read the following scriptures about grief:

    - Psalm 34:18
    - Matthew 5:4
    - Psalm 73:26
    - Revelations 21:4
    - Isaiah 53:4–6
    - Romans 2:8
    - Joshua 1:9
    - John 14:1

    What is the basic message from these scriptures about grief?

6. How does Mary's grief impact you?

7. How can Mary be a companion to you when you are grieving?

8. Mary is often referred to as the "seat of wisdom." What do you think this means?

Study Guide C

9. Grief is an important mental health concern. What is the percentage of people in the United States that are grieving each year?

10. Why is counseling an important choice to help people who are grieving?

11. Do you know someone who is grieving? How can you reach out to help them?

12. Mary is also known as Our Lady of Sorrows. What are the five sorrowful mysteries of the rosary? How do these mysteries relate to her? What days of the week do you pray the Sorrowful Mysteries?

Study Guide D

13. Create two more questions for this study guide.

14. Add two stanzas or four more lines to this poem. They may be added at the beginning of the poem, the middle, or the end of the poem.

15. Read the poem "Grief." Circle your favorite stanza. Why does it stir your heart?

16. Read the poem again. Circle a few words that stand out to you. Write a prayer to Jesus and include these words. Record the prayer in your journal to complete your personal book of prayers.

17. Play and sing your favorite songs or hymns about sorrow and grief.

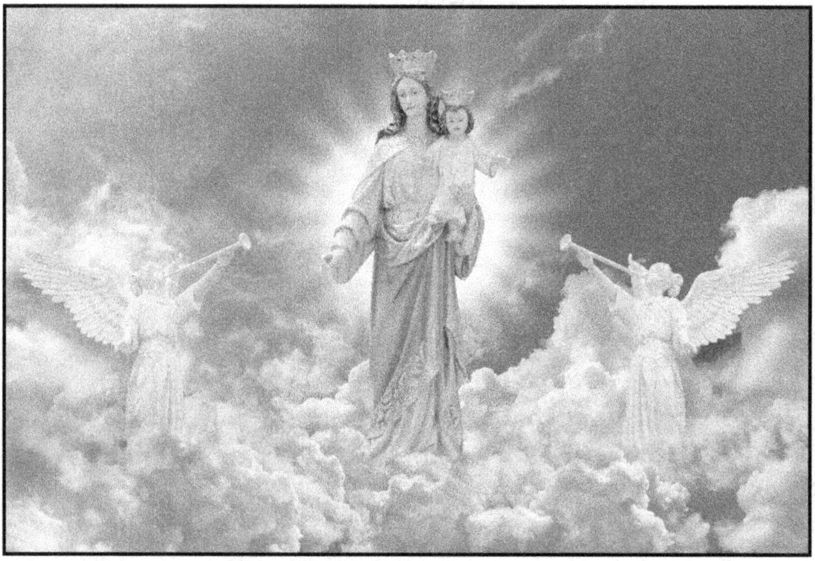

Mary, Queen of Heaven

Oh, Blessed Mother so holy and pure
God's gift to us you can rest assure.

A gift from heaven to help us here
By praying to you, we know you are near.

Please show us the way to your Son
And pray for us until it is done.

You are our Mother, full of grace
Can't wait to meet you one day face-to-face.

Mary, Queen of Heaven

Study Guide A

1. How is Mary a model of love?

2. How does Mary inspire us to trust God?

3. We love and honor Mary as our Queen of Heaven. Why do we honor Mary instead of worshiping her?

4. Record some ways in which we honor the Blessed Mother?

5. What is the history of the rosary? Explain the mysteries and the decades of the rosary. Each decade has a significant meaning. What are the meanings? Why are they important?

Study Guide B

6. Why is Mary considered to be the first step in finding your way to Jesus and God the Father?

7. What has God asked you to say yes to that you struggle with? How can Mary be an example to you to help you say yes?

8. Read the following scriptures from the Old Testament

    - Psalm 25:19
    - Deuteronomy 8:2
    - 1 Samuel 2:3
    - Proverbs 3:3–4
    What do these scriptures speak of?

Read the following scriptures in the New Testament. Locate the book and chapter. Now find the verse in each one that speaks of humility.

- James 4
- Luke 14
- Colossians 3
- Ephesians 4

9. Find three scriptures in the Old Testament and the New Testament that speak of poverty. What do these scriptures mean to you? Document them.

Study Guide C

10. Think about the virtues of humility and poverty that the Blessed Mother showed to others. How are these virtues in our own lives leading us to residing in heaven with her?

11. Think about spending eternity in heaven with the Blessed Mother. What does that look like to you?

12. Mary, crowned Queen of Heaven and Earth, is the fifth decade of the Luminous Mysteries of the rosary. Explain the Luminous Mysteries of the rosary. What do they stand for? What day do you pray the Luminous Mysteries of the rosary?

Study Guide D

13. Read the poem "Mary, Queen of Heaven." Circle the stanza that means the most to you. Why does it stir your heart?

14. Read the poem again. Circle several words that stand out to you. Write a prayer to Jesus, and include these words.

Record the prayer in your journal to complete your personal book of prayers.

15. Learn how to make string rosaries. You can find this on YouTube. Make and donate rosaries to a special group who needs them.

16. Play and sing your favorite songs or hymns about Mary, the Queen of Heaven.

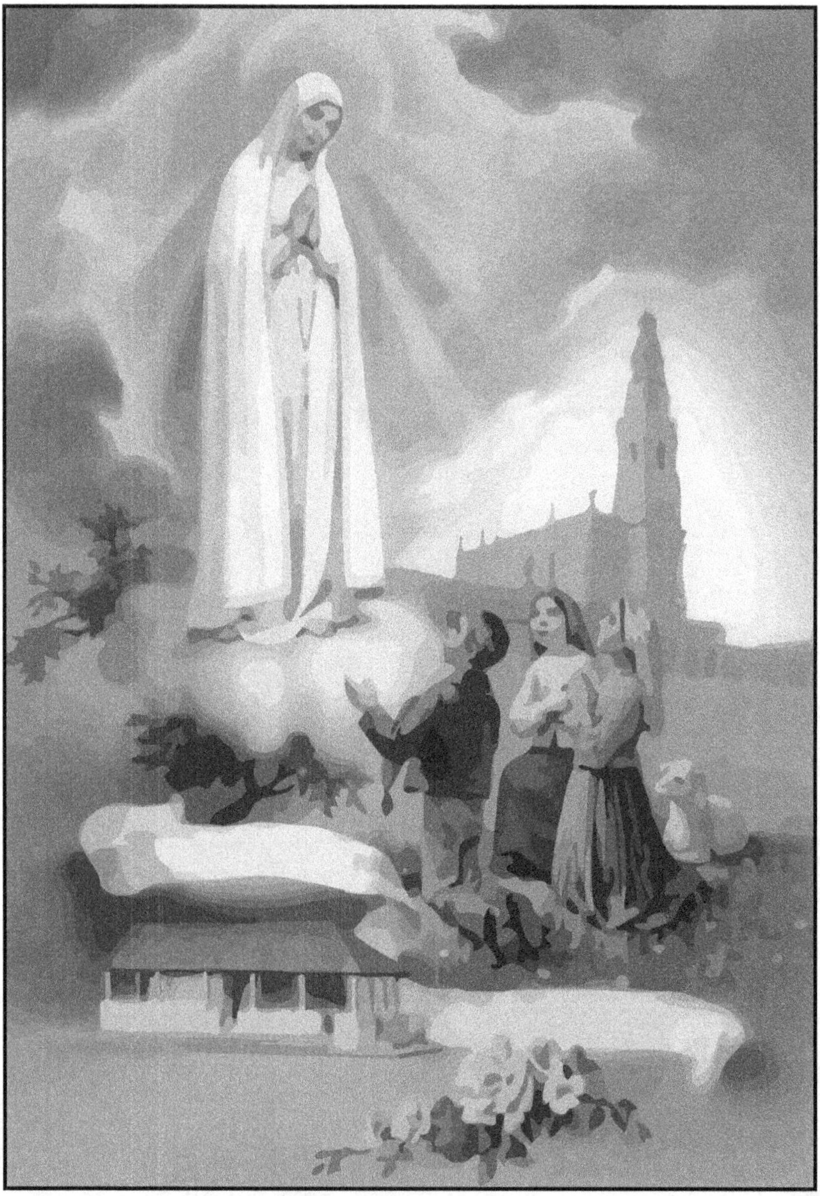

Prayer to Our Lady

O morning star, O dove of light
Come to our aid during this flight.

Give us the grace we need each day
To fight the world, for this we pray.

As a suckling babe in a mother's arms
Protect me from evil and all that harms.

Lead us to your Son most high
We can then say with a sigh
All praise and honor to God on high.

Prayer to Our Lady

Study Guide A

1. Read these scriptures about Mary. Luke 1:26–38 and Acts 1:14. What do these scriptures tell you about Mary?

2. Who is Our Lady to you?

3. What stands out the most about this image of Our Lady as related to this poem?

4. How is Mary the greatest role model for all Christians?

Study Guide B

5. How do you pray to the Blessed Mother?

6. What are the fifteen promises of Mary? What do they mean? How can they impact your life?

7. How have you allowed Our Lady to mother you?

8. How have you rested in the motherly arms of Mary?

Study Guide C

9. In this poem, it references "flight." Have you experienced a period of "flight" in your life? How can Our Lady be a part of rescuing you from that flight?

10. How can we relate to Mary in a very personal way that embodies her strength and willingness to say yes? If yes, how has she strengthened you? If not, what steps can you take to learn from her example?

11. What lessons can you learn from Mary that you can incorporate into your daily life that will help you on the road to heaven?

12. How do you think you would feel seeing Mary for the first time in heaven?

Study Guide D

13. When you pray the Hail Mary, describe the beauty and the scriptural truth. How does this relate to the rosary? Where are the words of the Hail Mary found in scripture?

14. Explain the Joyful Mysteries of the rosary. What do they stand for? What days of the week do you pray the Joyful mysteries?

15. Explain the Glorious Mysteries of the rosary. What do they stand for? What days of the week do you pray the Glorious Mysteries?

16. Read the poem "Prayer to Our Lady." Circle the paragraph that means the most to you. Why does it stir your heart?

17. Read the poem again. Circle a few words that stand out to you. Write a prayer to Jesus, and include these words. Record the prayer in your journal to complete your personal book of prayers.

18. Plan a party to honor the Blessed Mother. What food can you serve that is blue or can be tinted blue? For example, cupcakes with blue icing in the form of flowers.

19. Play and sing your favorite songs or hymns about Our Lady.

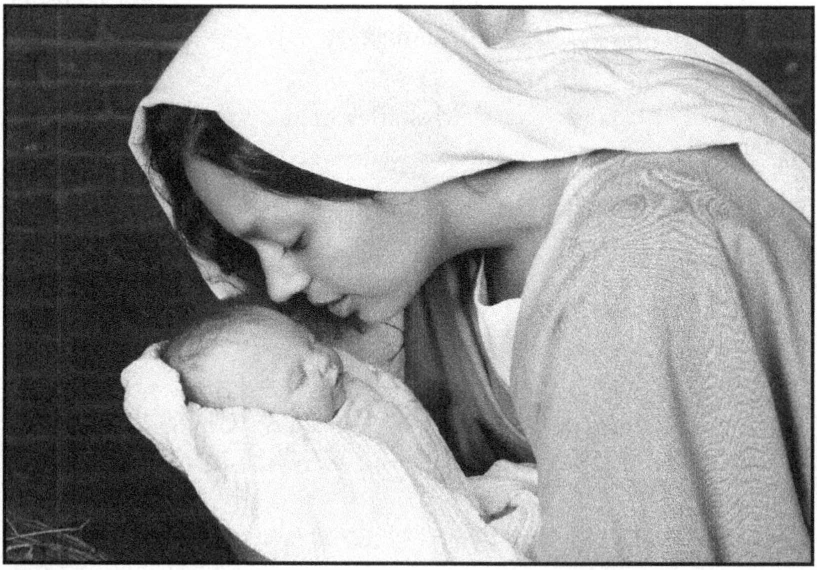

The Woman

A holy woman was chosen from birth
To bring her Son down to earth.

His name would be Jesus, a Savior for all
His love for us would lift us up after the fall.

A woman so holy with a love for man
She was put on earth to give us a helping hand.

A woman so holy and so pure
She will intercede for us, of that you can be sure.

So if we say these words at a graceful pace
To the woman we love, "Hail Mary, full of grace."

The Woman

Study Guide A

1. The Blessed Mother was chosen by God to be the vessel that would bring Jesus to us. How does that fact strengthen your love and honor for her?

2. What does "intercede" mean to you? How can Mary intercede for you?

3. Do you recognize the power in asking the Blessed Mother's intercession for us? How can we recognize her as the "gift from heaven" that she is?

4. Read Luke 1:41. Why did Mary's cousin Elizabeth call out to Mary when she saw her? What did she say?

5. Why was the miracle at Cana important to Mary and her son? What resulted from this?

Study Guide B

6. A way for us to find Jesus is through the Blessed Mother. What does that mean to you?

7. Why do we need Mary in our life? How has Mary impacted your life?

8. How can Mary's humanity make us more Christlike?

9. How can knowing Mary bring you joy and hope?

10. What are the symbols in the Immaculate Heart of Mary that shows us that she, too, is our mother who loves us and wants to lead us to her son? What do the symbols represent?

Study Guide C

11. Do you think God would refuse anything His mother would ask of Him? Why or why not?

12. Do you believe that you were chosen by God to also be a vessel that carries Jesus to others? If so, how can you do this?

13. Find and document three scriptures about evangelization in the New Testament.

14. Why was Paul such a successful evangelizer?

Study Guide D

15. Read John 19:26–27. What did Jesus command the other disciples to do as Mary looked on during the Crucifixion?

16. Read the poem "The Woman." Circle the paragraph that means the most to you. Why does it stir your heart?

17. Read the poem again. Write a prayer to Jesus, and include those words. Record the prayer in your journal to complete your personal book of prayers.

18. Play and sing your favorite songs or hymns about a woman.

Art Activity

To culminate this chapter, use your favorite art media to complete an original design that represents all the poems in chapter 5, "A Tribute to the Blessed Mother and Her Grief."

NOTES

NOTES

CHAPTER 6

The Resurrection

"I Am...the resurrected Lord."

He is not here for He has risen!

The Resurrection

O Jesus, our Savior, rose from the dead
Giving us grace to stay ahead.

He wants us all with Him above
We can make it happen with His mercy and love.

His father called Him from this life
To free Him from all hate and strife.

He made a place for Him by his side
A place where the Holy Spirit also resides.

Because of Christ's resurrection, we have been freed from sin
Making our hearts and souls pure and holy from within.

The Resurrection

Study Guide A

1. "The Resurrection" is the title of this poem. How does the title relate to the words "rose from the dead"? Why did Jesus ascend into heaven?

2. Describe what happened to Jesus three days before the Resurrection?

3. Read John 2:19–22 in the Bible. This refers to how Jesus told His disciples about the Resurrection. Why did He say "Destroy this temple and in three days. I will raise it up"?

4. Who was Mary Magdalene? What do you know about her reputation? Why was she upset at the tomb on Easter morning?

Study Guide B

5. Jesus first appeared to Mary Magdalene when He rose from the dead. Why did Jesus appear to her first?

6. What did Mary Magdalene do when she first saw Jesus out of the tomb?

7. What did Thomas do when he first saw Jesus out of the tomb?

8. Are you more like Mary Magdalene or Thomas? Explain.

Study Guide C

9. How does the Resurrection relate to us today?

10. Take a moment to reflect on lines 3 and 4 of "The Resurrection" poem. In what ways does God help us be with Him in His mercy and love? How is the sacrament of reconciliation (confession) tied to this?

11. Find some examples in the Old Testament and the New Testament where people were resurrected—raised from the dead. Document them.

Study Guide D

12. Read the poem "The Resurrection." Circle the stanza that stands out to you. Why does it move you?

13. Read the poem again. Circle a few words that stand out to you. Write a prayer to Jesus, and include these words. Record the prayer in your journal to complete your personal book of prayers.

14. Play and sing your favorite songs or hymns about the Resurrection.

15. Go to yourhomebasedmom.com. Follow this recipe to bake resurrection cookies, also known as Empty Tomb cookies. With your children, follow the directions step-by-step and recall how each step of baking relates to the Crucifixion and the Resurrection. Enjoy the cookies Easter morning!

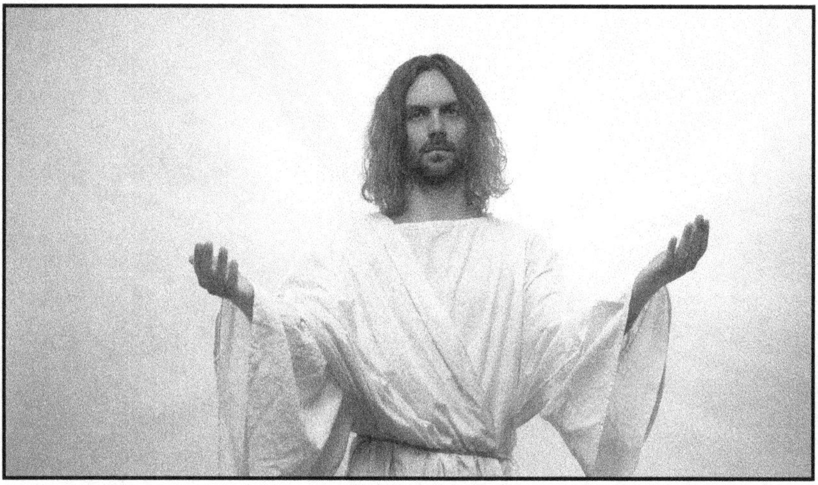

Welcome Home

For those who are lost and have gone astray
Ask for God's help to come back to stay.

Get on your knees and ask for His grace
To come back home at a rapid pace.

The ways of the world can pull you away
You can lose all you have in just one day.

Store up your treasures for eternal life
Give up those things that cause you strife.

The end will come for you one day
When you face the Lord, what will you say?

Did you feed the hungry, or send them away?
Did you clothe the naked and ask them to stay?

If you did all of these things with a tender love
Your place is with Him in heaven above.

Welcome Home

Study Guide A

1. There are two parts to this poem. One is personal, and one relates to other people. Why are they both important?

2. What are the "ways of the world" that can pull us away from God?

3. The Bible says to store your treasures in heaven? What is your heavenly treasure?

Study Guide B

4. What are some things in your life you should give up that cause you strife?

5. What can you do if you have done or said something that you are later sorry for?

6. Read Matthew 25:31–40 and Isaiah 58:1–9. What are the Corporal Works of Mercy?

Study Guide C

7. In what ways can you use the poem "Welcome Home" to practice the Corporal Works of Mercy in your life? How do these works help us to minister to the hearts and souls of our neighbors?

8. Below are listed the Spiritual Works of Mercy. Also included is a book and chapter in the Bible that denotes this special act. Find the scriptural verses for each one. Document them.

- Counsel the doubtful—Proverbs 19 and 1 Corinthians 1
- Instruct the ignorant—Hosea 4 and Romans 2
- Admonishing the sinner—Mathew 7 and Psalm 141
- Comforting the sorrowful—Hebrew 13 and John 16
- Forgiving injuries—Matthew 18 and Psalm 32.
- Praying for the living and the dead—Numbers 12 and John 17

9. Which of the above scriptures are from the Old Testament and which are from the New Testament?

Study Guide D

10. Read the poem "Welcome Home." Which stanza stands out to you? Why does it move you?

11. Read the poem again. Circle a few words that stand out to you. Write a prayer to Jesus, and include these words. Record this prayer in your journal to complete your personal book of prayers.

12. Make a list of three people who need your help, at this time, using the Corporal Works of Mercy or the Spiritual Works of Mercy. Who are they, and what do they need? Have you reached out to them?

13. Play and sing your favorite songs or hymns about welcome home.

Your Soul Lives On

The Soul

If we could only see the soul
I'm sure it would be a sight to behold.

At the moment of conception
Our soul was given to us without exception.

The soul, a gift from God to everyone
Even to the unborn, the little one.

The soul is also brightly white
But the sins of man can put it to flight.

So if we confess our sins and change our ways
We can be sure of eternal life in heaven one day.

The Soul

Study Guide A

1. Why do we say that the soul is an abstract concept? How is it possible to not see the soul but know that is exists?

2. Biblically, what is the difference between the soul and the spirit? Explain.

3. What proves that Jesus had the power to heal a person's soul? Find some examples in scripture. Document them.

Study Guide B

4. If the soul is immortal, how does the existence of the soul relate to heaven?

5. There has been much controversy about "How soon does life begin in the womb?" How would the author of this poem answer that question? How would you answer it?

6. Explain the steps of committing sin, confession, and repentance as they relate to the soul. What sacrament is this related to? Why?

7. St. Paul uses the Greek word *soul* in the New Testament. This word means "breath." Read Genesis 2:7. Reflect again on the poem "The Soul." What does this now mean to you?

Study Guide C

8. Read the following scriptures in the Old Testament. First, read the chapters listed below. Then find the verse in each one that speaks of the soul.

- Deuteronomy 4
- Psalm 42
- Jeremiah 6
- Psalm 19

   What do they mean to you? Document them.

9. Read the following scripture in the New Testament. First, read the chapter listed below. Then find the verse that speaks of the soul.

   - Matthew 22
   - Matthew 10

   What do they mean to you? Document them.

10. Add two more questions to this study guide about the soul.

Study Guide D

11. Read the poem "The Soul." Which stanza means the most to you? Why does it move you?

12. Read the poem again. Circle a few words that stand out to you. Write a prayer to Jesus, and include these words. Record the prayer in your journal to complete your personal book of prayers.

13. Prepare and eat your favorite "soul" food.

14. Find and sing your favorite songs or hymns about the soul.

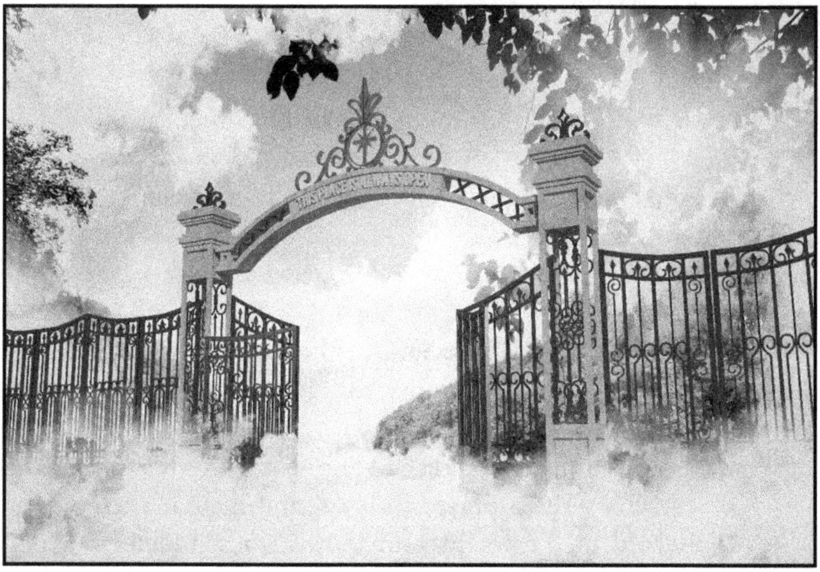

The Kingdom

Our Lord and Savior came down to earth
Opening the gates of His kingdom by His birth.

The kingdom is a place we all want to be
A place of beauty we all need to see.

His love for us is ever so great
If we follow His will, it will never be too late.

By His death and resurrection, He opened the door
Because of His mercy, we were given a chance once more.

So to be with Him in His kingdom above
We should treat all people with His kind of love.

The Kingdom

Study Guide A

1. How would you describe God's kingdom?

2. Read these Bible verses from the Old Testament:

   - Micah 4:3
   - Isaiah 32:1
   - Hebrews 12:28
   - Psalm 45:6

   Using these scriptures, describe God's kingdom. What do they mean to you?

3. Read these scriptures from the New Testament:

   - Mark 1:5
   - Luke 12:32
   - Matthew 6:33
   - Revelations 11:15

   Using these scriptures, describe God's kingdom. What do they mean to you? How are the Old Testament and New Testament scriptures connected?

Study Guide B

4. If it were up to you, how would you build the kingdom of God?

5. In Matthew 19:13–15, God proposes that the kingdom of God belongs to those who are like children. What does He mean? Explain.

6. Read the book of Luke 17:21. What does it mean when Jesus said the kingdom is within you?

7. How do we experience the kingdom of God? How can we teach this to others?

8. To enter the kingdom of God, we have several requirements. What are they? Explain.

Study Guide C

9. What is God's kind of love?

10. How do we show His kind of love to others?

11. When you pray the Our Father, what does "thy kingdom come, thy will be done" mean to you?

12. Because of Jesus's death and resurrection, we were saved. How did this happen? What does that mean to you?

Study Guide D

13. Read the poem "The Kingdom." Circle the paragraph that means the most to you. Why does it move you?

14. Write two more stanzas or four more lines to the poem. You may add them at the beginning, middle, or end of the poem.

15. Read the poem again. Circle a few words that stand out to you. Write a prayer to Jesus, and include these words. Record the prayer in your journal to complete your personal book of prayers.

16. Play and sing your favorite songs or hymns about the kingdom of God.

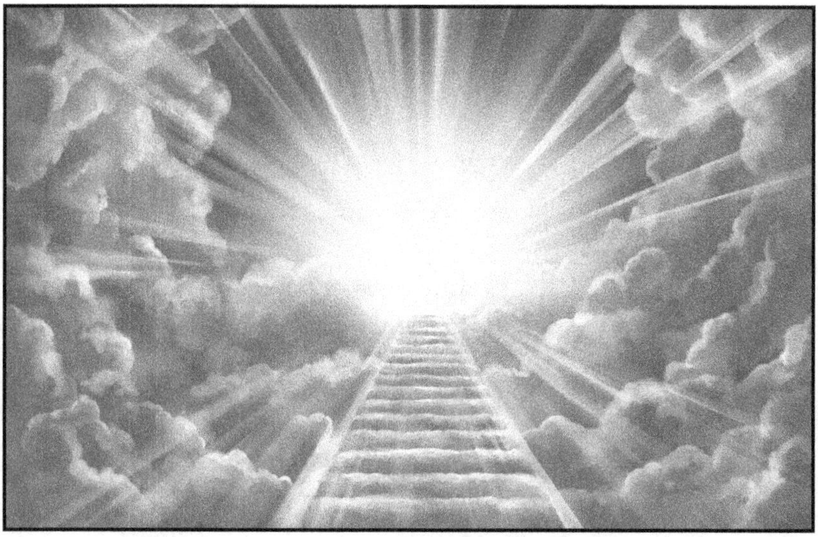

Heaven

When angels sing
and trumpets blare,

We know for sure
God is always there.

The streets are paved
with silver and gold,

As was mentioned
Many times long ago.

We picture God sitting
on His throne,

Waiting for us to
eventually come home.

As He sits on His throne
Looking down from above,

He will gather all His people
Because of His love.

You can rest assure
If you follow His way,

Trials and tribulations
Will come to you one day.

So if you get down on your knees
And look His way,

Pray to be with Him
in heaven one day.

Heaven

Study Guide A

1. If you hear angels sing and trumpets blare, where do you think you are? Why?

2. How would you describe heaven? Who do you think you will see there?

3. What does science say about heaven?

Study Guide B

4. What does science say about silver and gold?

5. Why were silver and gold so important during biblical times?

6. Find four scriptures in the Old Testament and four scriptures in the New Testament that speak of silver and gold. Document them.

Study Guide C

7. What do we call "the throne of God" on earth?

8. Find four Bible scriptures about the throne of God. Document them. What do they tell you about the throne of God?

9. What have been your trials and tribulations this past week? How did you cope with them?

10. How does prayer help us to be with Him in heaven one day?

Study Guide D

11. Read the poem "Heaven." Circle the stanza that attracts you. Why does this part of the poem stir your heart?

12. Read the poem again. Circle several words that stand out to you. Write a prayer to Jesus, and include these words. Record the prayer in your journal to complete your personal book of prayers.

13. Create two more questions for this study guide.

14. Play and sing your favorite songs or hymns about heaven.

Art Activity

To culminate this chapter, use your favorite art media to complete an original design that represents the poems in chapter 6, "The Resurrection."

NOTES

NOTES

CHAPTER 7

The Descent of the Holy Spirit

"I Am...the Holy Spirit—present with you always."

Come Holy Spirit

COME, HOLY SPIRIT

O Holy Spirit, come down from above
Give us gifts and gentle love.
Come to our aid with a helping hand
To pray and praise the best we can.

Help us to fight the enemy here
And let us know that You are near.
Our flesh is weak, our hearts seek to be strong
Please keep us from sinning
And doing what's wrong.

Show us the way to the Father and Son
That we may worship God, three in one.
Blessed Trinity, the name we call
A mystery from heaven for one and all.

Come, Holy Spirit

Study Guide A

1. Who is the Holy Spirit to you? Read the five scriptures below. Who is the Holy Spirit in each scripture?

    - John 16:7
    - John 3:16
    - 1 Corinthians 12:3
    - John 16:18–19
    - John 16:12–14

2. What are the seven gifts of the Holy Spirit? Explain each one. Find a Bible scripture that corresponds with each one.

3. How do you make yourself worthy to receive the gifts of the Holy Spirit?

4. What gifts of the Holy Spirit are strongest in you?

Study Guide B

5. The author says that we must "fight the enemy here." Ephesians 6 speaks of taking up the armor of God to fight evil. Read in Ephesians 6:10–17. What is included in the armor of God?

6. How do we ask God to equip us with the armor we need?

7. Which article of armor are you in most need of today? Why?

Study Guide C

8. How does the Holy Spirit guide us away from sin to lead a Christian life?

9. Why is the Blessed Trinity referred to as a mystery?

10. How would you use an egg to explain the Blessed Trinity? What else could be used to describe the Blessed Trinity in a simple way using the three in one concept?

Study Guide D

11. Read the poem "Come, Holy Spirit." Circle the stanza that means the most to you. Why does it move you?

12. Read the poem again. Circle a few words that stand out to you. Write a prayer to Jesus, and include these words. Record the prayer in your journal to complete your personal book of prayers.

13. Add two more questions to this study guide.

14. Play and sing your favorite songs about "Come, Holy Spirit."

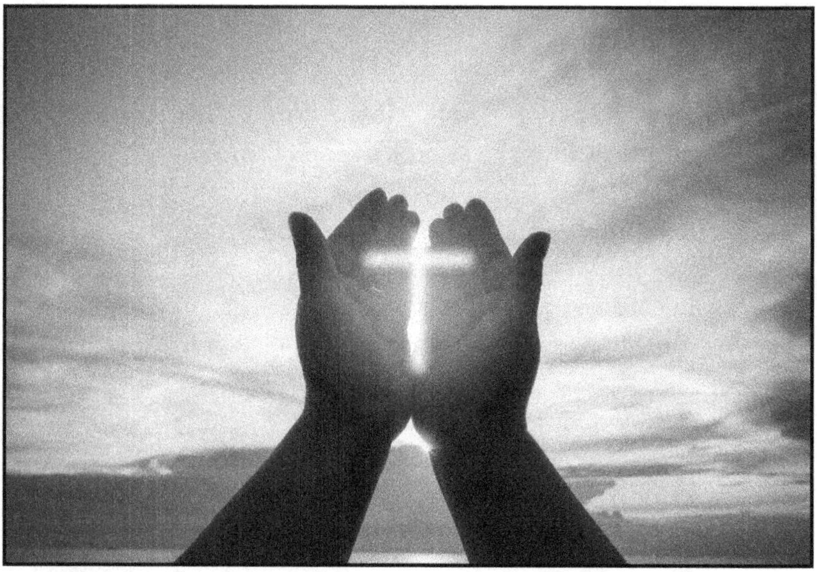

The Spirit of God

Oh, Holy Spirit, with God so near
Came down from heaven to be with us here.

He came to us to give us grace
To help us each day to see him face to face.

As we walk this earth looking for love
Just raise your head and look above.

You will receive graces necessary for life
To overcome trouble, temptation, and strife.

So as we pass through this life to reach the kingdom above
We know for sure we will meet our God of love.

The Spirit of God

Study Guide A

1. Who is the Holy Spirit? Read the four Bible scriptures below. Who is the Holy Spirit in each scripture?

    - John 15:26
    - Acts 1:4–5
    - Galatians 5:22–23
    - Galatians 5:16–17

2. We usually think of the Holy Spirit coming to us in a form of a dove. However, the Holy Spirit has come to us in several other forms. Read the following scriptures, and record the way the Holy Spirit is coming in each scripture.

    - Matthew 3:16–17
    - Ephesians 1:13–14
    - 1 Samuel 16:13
    - Luke 3:16–17
    - Acts 2:2–5
    - John 3:5
    - Hosea 6:3
    - Psalm 1:3
    - Acts 2: 13–17

3. On Pentecost Sunday, how did the Holy Spirit descend upon the apostles? What forms did He take?

Study Guide B

4. How can we be filled with the Holy Spirit?

5. The gifts of the Holy Spirit include

- wisdom
- knowledge
- understanding
- counsel
- fortitude
- piety and
- fear of the Lord

What does each gift mean to you? What is your strongest gift?

6. How can you use the gifts of the Holy Spirit to help others? Give examples.

Study Guide C

7. How are the gifts of the Holy Spirit linked from the Old Testament to the New Testament?

8. Read the poem "The Spirit of God." Circle the stanza that stands out to you. Why does it stir your heart?

9. Read the poem again. Circle a few words that stand out to you. Write a prayer to Jesus, and include these words. Record the prayer in your journal to complete your personal book of prayers.

Study Guide D

10. Add two more stanzas or four more lines to this poem. They may be added at the beginning, middle, or end of the poem.

11. Add two more questions to this study guide.

12. Play and sing your favorite songs or hymns about the spirit of God.

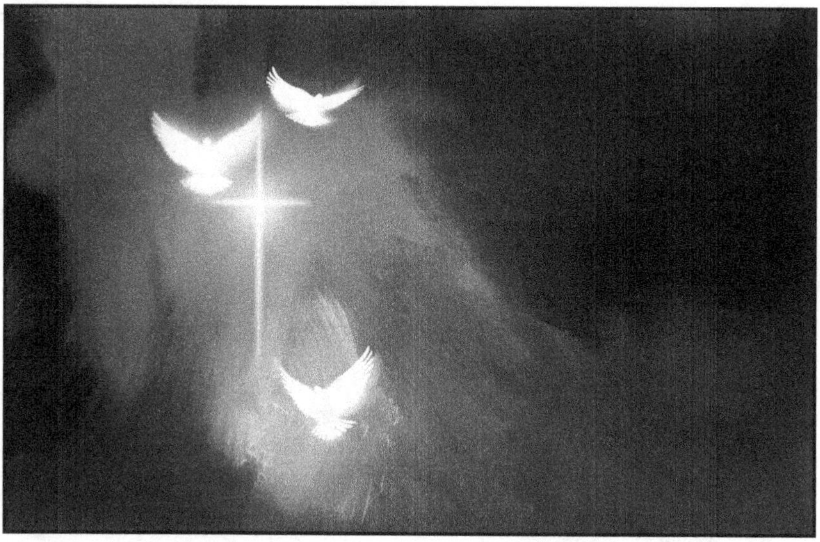

Thank You, Holy Spirit

O Holy Spirit, a light from above
Come to me as a gentle dove.

As I lay in my bed sound asleep
I pray to God my soul to keep.

He is always with me during the day
Giving me graces to follow His way.

I may stumble and fall along the way
But my place in heaven is where I will stay.

So I thank you Holy Spirit for all you have done
Helping me to meet God one on one.

Thank You, Holy Spirit

Study Guide A

1. Define the Holy Spirit. Read the Bible scriptures below. Who is the Holy Spirit in each scripture? Record your answers.

    - Romans 8:5–6
    - 2 Corinthians 3:17–18

2. Why do we need the Holy Spirit in our lives?

3. How does the Holy Spirit help us strengthen our belief in God?

4. Why would this poem be a good prayer for the end of the day?

Study Guide B

5. The fruits of the Holy Spirit are the following:

    - Love
    - Joy
    - Peace
    - Patience
    - Kindness
    - Generosity
    - Faithfulness
    - Gentleness
    - Self-Control

    Find a Bible verse from the Old Testament and one from the New Testament that describe each one. Document them.

6. How do we use the fruits of the Holy Spirit in our daily lives to help others?

7. What is the quality of fruits you have in your life? Do you feel you are growing closer to God or farther away?

8. What is the difference between the gifts of the Holy Spirit and the fruits of the Holy Spirit?

Study Guide C

9. How is the Holy Spirit present in the sacraments? Find your answer in scripture. Document it.

10. How will the Holy Spirit help us in assuring our salvation?

11. Do you know a Christian that you believe is not filled with the Holy Spirit? How can you encourage them?

12. Read the poem "Thank you, Holy Spirit." Circle the paragraph that moves your heart. Why does it speak to you?

Study Guide D

13. Read the poem again. Circle a few words that stand out to you. Write a prayer to Jesus, and include these words. Record your prayer in your journal to complete your personal book of prayers.

14. Add two more questions about the Holy Spirit to this study guide.

15. Play and sing your favorite songs or hymns about the Holy Spirit.

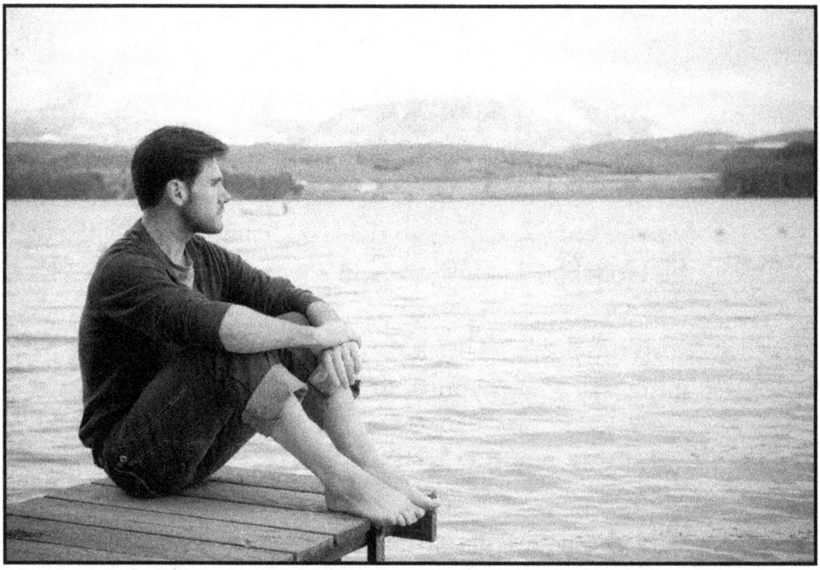

My Life

As I sit here and look at my life
I can now see things that caused me strife.

I prayed to God to lift me up
And that one day I could drink from His cup.

He sent me the Holy Spirit, the dove
And also the graces to see His love.

He kept His word and showed me the way
I will pray to be with Him one day.

Because of His mercy I know I will win
Hoping to be with Him in heaven in the end.

My Life

Study Guide A

1. When Jesus was crucified, God said HE would send someone to take HIS place. HE sent the Holy Spirit. How have you let the Holy Spirit guide you in your life? What were the results?

2. When we keep out word, we are practicing faithfulness. Find two scriptures from the Old Testament and two scriptures from the New Testament that speak of being faithful.

3. How have you practiced faithfulness to your friends and family?

Study Guide B

4. What is the greatest hope we have that we will be in heaven with our Lord at the end of our life?

5. How does the Holy Spirit make us more Christlike? Read Romans 8:15–16 and explain.

6. How does the Holy Spirit give us power to witness? Read Acts 1:8 and 2 Timothy 1:7 and explain.

7. How does the Holy Spirit guide us to all truths? Read John 16:18–19 and Romans 8:14–16 and explain.

Study Guide C

8. How does the Holy Spirit convict us of all sin?

9. How does the Holy Spirit reveal God's word to us? Read 2 Timothy 3:16 and John 14:26. Document your answers.

10. How does the Holy Spirit bring us closer to other believers? Read Acts 4:32. Document your answers.

11. Read the poem "My Life." Circle the paragraph that moves you. Why does it stir your heart?

Study Guide D

12. Read the poem again. Circle a few words that stand out to you. When you are ready, write a prayer to Jesus, and include these words. Record the prayer in your journal to complete your personal book of prayers.

13. Add two more questions to this study guide.

14. Play and sing your favorite songs or hymns about "My Life."

Art Activity

To culminate this chapter, use your favorite art media to complete an original design that represents the poems in chapter 7, "The Descent of the Holy Spirit."

REFERENCES

Books

A Cardiologist Examines Jesus: The Stunning Science behind Eucharistic Miracles
Dr. Franco Serafina

Basic Elements of the Catholic Church
Dr. Peter Kreeft, PhD
Ignatius Press. First Edition. March 1, 2001.

Seven Secrets of the Eucharist
Vinny Flynn
Introduction by Fr. Mitch Pacwa, SJ
Published by Mercy Song Inc. Stonebridge, Massachusetts, in collaboration with Ignatius Press. December 2006.

The Greatest Philosopher That Ever Lived
Peter Kreeft
Ignatius Press. 2021.
The Physics of Angels: Exploring the Realm Where Science and Spirit Meet
Matthew Fox and Rupert Sheldrake
Monkfish Publishing. 2014.

Twelve Undeniable Facts that Prove the Resurrection
Dr. Bob Martin

The New American Bible (1976)
The New King James Version
The English Standard Version

Magazines

The Word Among Us
Daily Meditations (January, February, March, April, May, June, July, August 2022)

Photographs

Shutterstock Images

Videos

Eucharist Miracles: Scientific Proof that Eucharist is the Body of Christ
Dr. Taylor Marshall
Interviewed by Ray Grijalba

Websites

artincontext.org
bible.knowing-jesus.com
biblesforamerica.org
biblegateway.com
biblestudytools.com (Clarence L. Haynes Jr.)
catholicdigest.com
catholicweekly.com
christianity.com
countryliving.com
crosswalk.com
dailyverses.net
denvercatholic.org
ewtn.com
gotquestions.org
ibelieve.com (Kingdom of God)
kingjamesbibleonline.org
openbible.info
teachingwhereyourecalled.com

thecatholicspirit.com
youtube.com
yourhomebasedmom.com

Resource People

Tammy Bernard
Monica Broussard
Drew and Anne Marie Chesher
Sandra Cooley
Brandee Cordova
Cindy Moss Dowden
George and Lisa Hardy
Mimi Hardy
Linda Harris
Gwen Terrell Johnson
Martha H. Koury
Pat and Cynthia Lamitina
Chad and Sandy LeBeouff
Claire Lemoine
Father Kenneth Michiels
Mike Mitcham
Monica Nicholson
Shirley Quinones
Roisin Renz
Jan Scoles
Gloria Shelby
Barbara Stainback
Lynn and Steve Stephen
Jackie Vaughan
Craig and Jonette Whitley

ABOUT THE AUTHORS

Marcus Descant was born and raised in Alexandria, Louisiana. He graduated high school in 1958 and completed a bachelor of science degree in pharmacy from Northeast State University (now ULM) in Monroe, Louisiana in 1963. He has been a practicing pharmacist for fifty-eight years.

In the 1980s, he was inspired to write prayer poems. The prayer poems he writes are for all Christians. The poems came slowly for many years. Then a few years ago, he felt the need to write them more often.

He married his wife, Liz, in 2001. They founded Holy Trinity Ministries of Louisiana in 2016. Liz is a retired teacher and school administrator.

They visit prayer groups, churches, and schools sharing their ministry.

He now has forty prayer poems. Over the years, he had the poems printed on cards and gave them away by the thousands. So many people kept asking him to publish a book. He and his wife decided they would.

His wife, Liz, and him live in Leesville, Louisiana. He continues to work as a pharmacist part time while writing prayer poems and sharing their ministry. Between the couple are five children and twenty-two grandchildren and great-grandchildren. They have a busy and blessed life!